GUINEA PIGS
Technologies of Control

GUINEA PIGS

Technologies of Control

by
John Hall

Strategic Book Publishing and Rights Co.

Strategic Book Publishing and Rights Co.
12620 FM 1960, Suite A4-507
Houston, TX 77065
www.sbpra.com

For information about special discounts for bulk purchases, please contact Strategic Book Publishing and Rights Co. Special Sales, at bookorder@sbpra.net

ISBN: 978-1-63135-552-3

Book Design by Julius Kiskis

21 22 20 19 18 17 16 15 14   1 2 3 4 5

DEDICATION

This book is dedicated to the memory of Dr. Fred Bell,
a true patriot and good friend.

Contents

PREFACE

Since the dawn of civilization man has turned his attention inward to harness the power of the mind and expand, explain and potentially control his environment. As early as the Paleolithic period, man turned to the shaman for explanations regarding fertility, the environment and healing. These shamans supposedly possessed the ability to connect to spiritual realms as well as the natural energies of the universe, allowing them to help with matters that may have been afflicting the entire tribe. One looks no further than writings about North American medicine men to see accurate illustrations of the power attributed to these Native American shamans. D.D Mitchell, superintendent of Indian Affairs in the 1800's, documented his experience with the Bear Medicine Men of the Arikara tribe. Mitchell and several other white men were invited to take part in the Bear Medicine Men ceremony at the Arikara during which the medicine men, dressed like bears, would demonstrate their power to the non-believing white men. In his journal he detailed how the medicine men took clay and fashioned tiny horses, buffalo, and warriors, complete with tiny bows and arrows from the clay. The figurines were placed in a circle drawn into the dirt floor at the lodge. Upon the spoken command of one of the medicine men the clay figurines became animate, each warrior on horseback chasing down the buffalo and shooting arrows into them. After the clay figurines finished their hunt, they were further instructed to ride into the fire that was placed in the center of the circle. The baked clay figurines were then crushed into dust and the dust handed to D.D. Mitchell. After a careful search of the lodge and the medicine men, Mitchell could not identify any means by which the demonstration was accomplished. In his journal he attributed their ability to animate the clay figurines to some sort of witchcraft or demonic force. Many other actions performed by medicine men were recorded by other Indian Affairs employees and Jesuit priests. Perhaps the easiest explanation would be that the medicine men possessed a tremendous ability to successfully hypnotize the spectators.

The term hypnosis was coined by a Scottish surgeon named James Braid who based his practice on the techniques developed by Franz Mesmer, the first to describe Animal Magnetism. According to Mesmer, there is a natural energetic transference that occurs between all animate and inanimate objects that results in energy movement through channels in the body. For those readers familiar with basic quantum physics, this theory should look very familiar. It is essentially an early, crude description of the Einstein–Podolsky–Rosen Theory. Eventually hypnosis was taken seriously by psychological and parapsychological researchers and seen as more than a parlor trick.

As research into hypnosis and other forms of ESP took root in the scientific and medical communities, the government began to take notice. Nonconsensual medical experimentation was already rampant in most industrialized countries, including the United States. The secret of unlocking the human mind was irresistible to these doing military research for most governments. As Korean prisoners of war returned from China showing signs of brainwashing, the race for learning the techniques for controlling the human mind began. The creation of Manchurian Candidates, individuals who can be controlled in an altered personality state, was deemed a necessity by both the DOD and intelligence agencies. Unfortunately, the search for viable control technologies has resulted in a plethora of nonconsensual experimentation that has continued into current day.

Acknowledgments

Special thanks to Jennifer Shannon. Over the past five years she has learned a lot about this technology, has been by my side meeting with many TI's and spent countless hours working on this book. Without her commitment to this project, and putting my notes into type, this would not be in print today.

CHAPTER 1

Non – Consensual Experimentation

"Fracture for Fracture, Eye for Eye, Tooth for Tooth; whatever
injury he has given a person shall be given to him."
–Leviticus 24:30

When one speaks of nonconsensual experimentation, the immediate picture one gets in their mind is a Nazi camp where grotesque experiments were carried out on imprisoned Jews. Most Americans have no clue that many of the doctors carrying out those experiments were brought to the United States, bypassing the Nuremberg trials, by the Office of Strategic Services through Operation Paperclip. Many others were assisted out of Germany, prior to the fall of Berlin, by the Catholic Church who supplied them with false passports to South American countries like Uruguay and Paraguay. The strides they had made through nonconsensual experimentation were seen as a rationale to the national security of the United States. As a matter of fact, until recently, the Aerospace Library at Randolph Air Force Base in San Antonio, Texas was named the Strughold Aerospace Library, named after Hubertus Strughold He is widely known as the Father of American Aerospace Medicine for his role in pioneering manned space flight. Before being brought to the United States under Operation Paperclip, he was a Colonel in the Luftwaffe as a senior advisor in their medical service overseeing medical experimentation. The Luftwaffe Medical Service used Dachau concentration camp prisoners as test subjects in experiments that included immersion in freezing water, pressure chamber testing, forced seawater intake and invasive surgery without anesthesia. At the Nuremberg trials Strughold contributed several affidavits on behalf of his research assistant, Hermann Becker-Freyseng, who was convicted of crimes against humanity despite Strughold's defense. All told, over 1600 psychiatrists, medical doctors and physicists were brought to the US to continue their work.

Nazi Germany first saw the use of psychiatry as a punitive tool for controlling political dissidents. Psychiatry is uniquely positioned as the perfect tool to enforce political obedience through confinement of those who disagree with current government policy. In Nazi Germany, psychiatrists were responsible for killing hundreds of thousands of their patients deemed racially and cognitively compromised. Psychiatrists led the way in brainwashing and mind control experiments and were highly sought after as Operation Paperclip transferees. They were allowed to continue their mind control research in the United States under the auspices of the newly formed Central Intelligence Agency after World War II. Unfortunately, psychiatry has continued to be used punitively to this day in all countries and an entire chapter is dedicated to this questionable medical practice later in this book.

The nonconsensual experimentation being done in Nazi Germany was not done in a microcosm; much of it was in direct replication of experimentation already being done in the United States. The atrocities in the concentration camps were a reflection of atrocities being committed here in the name of furthering medical science. For example, it is widely held that the

Nazi eugenics programs were adopted from eugenics programs already in place in the United States. According to a Yale study, the popular movement aimed at improving society through selective breeding, indicates that forced sterilizations were carried out on a much larger and longer scale than previously believed, beginning with the first eugenics law passed in Indiana in 1907. Eugenics or Social Darwinism, today known as social engineering, suggested that science can engineer progress by attacking social ills like moral decadence, crime, venereal disease and alcoholism with forced sterilization. A year after Hitler took power, the New England Journal of Medicine in 1943 praised Germany as "the most progressive nation in restricting fecundity among the unfit." Forced sterilization was legal in 18 states in the US until the 1960's, with sterilization possible without consent. Moreover, in 1926, Supreme Court Justice Oliver Wendell Holmes wrote, "It is better for all of the world, if instead of waiting to execute degenerate offspring for crime, or to let them starve for their imbecility, society can prevent those who are manifestly unfit from continuing their kind." While most eugenics laws in the United States were eliminated by the 1960's, resurgence in the institution of eugenics has rooted itself within the Obama Administration. Many of the "czars" he appointed after his initial election are devout eugenicists. Social engineering attempts of this administration have included health care rationing to the elderly, death panels to determine who may be too ill to keep on life support, late-term abortion, the reinstitution of forced sterilization, forced abortion and administration of birth control to girls as young as 14 years of age without the need for parental consent. Not having learned a lesson from past atrocities, progressives in our current government are still determined to create the society that they feel is best for us based on their elitist attitudes and disdain for those intelligent enough to question their motives. Unfortunately, a vast percentage of Americans under the age of thirty have been successfully dumbed-down by federally mandated public school curriculum to not possess the ability to question the government about anything. Assuming this book is written on a 10th grade level or better, consider yourself in the minority if you are understanding it since 90% of adults in the United States read between the 8th and 9th grade level.

Understanding the extent of nonconsensual experimentation that has taken place in this country is integral to understanding the arguments made throughout the rest of this book. It is a bitter pill to swallow among the most patriotic and ethical among us, but a necessary topic to grasp. While the United States has been most vocal and critical of human rights abuses in other countries, we have a horrible track record ourselves that has continued into present day. Some of the more glaring examples of nonconsensual experimentation will be presented here and my point will be made and will probably be troubling to many readers. Unfortunately, there is no legislation in the United States that prevents government agencies from experimenting on the public. Ethicists point to two documents as a safeguard against nonconsensual experimentation, the Nuremberg Code and the Common Rule. However, the Nuremberg Code is merely a suggestion and not a recognized law and the Common Rule is route with loopholes allowing for experimentation despite its lengthy read. After a reporter brought to light United States sponsored experimentation on Guatemalan prisoners, Secretary of State Hilary Clinton apologized to the people of Guatemala and President Obama appointed the Bioethics Commission to determine if any other experimentation is ongoing. The experimentation in Guatemala took place from 1946-1949 during which the United States Public Health Service intentionally infected Guatemalan prisoners with syphilis, gonorrhea and chancroid. In 2011 the Bioethics Commission convened four meetings to address current safeguards against nonconsensual human experimentation. I spoke at the first meeting and was the only physician to present the inadequacy of the Common Rule to prevent nonconsensual experimentation. The commission itself was largely comprised of apologists for the government, although their final report did call for stronger legislation. Of note, at each meeting, greater than 100 people were there at the public forum voicing complaints of nonconsensual experimentation with directed energy and electromagnetic weapons. The number of individuals voicing these complaints grew so large by the fourth meeting that the Chairman of the Commission, Amy Gutmann, asked that individuals complaining of directed energy research not attend.

A very brief and incomplete history of nonconsensual experimentation sponsored by the United States Government agencies is included here for the reader. After reading this history and researching it yourself, the complaints that are currently being voiced on experimentation with technologies of control should not seem so unfathomable.

1919-1922: Testicular transplant experimentation on five hundred prisoners at San Quentin.

1927: Carrie Buck was legally sterilized against her will in Charlottesville, Virginia. She was the mentally sound daughter of a mentally retarded mother who was sterilized under eugenics laws of the era. Buck vs. Bell upheld the legality of her sterilization but has been criticized in legal circles ever since.

1931: Dr. Cornelius Rhoads conducts cancer experiments on Puerto Rican subjects by injecting them with cancer cells under the auspices of the Rockefeller Institute for Medical Investigations. Rhoads was also responsible for later radiation experiments. The American Association for Cancer Research honored him by naming an award after him.

1932-1972: United States Public Health Service and The Tuskegee Institute in Alabama test syphilis bacteria on 400 poor black share-croppers. They were repeatedly refused treatment and experimentation only ended after a reporter brought it to light.

1946-1953: Atomic Energy Commission feeds residents at the Fernald School in Massachusetts irradiated Quaker Oats to study effects of radiation.

1949: Intentional release of iodine 131 and xenon 133 over Hartford, Washington by Atomic Energy Commission in a study called "Green Run."

1950: Dr. Joseph Stokes from the University of Pennsylvania deliberately infects 200 female prisoners with viral hepatitis.

1951-1960: University of Pennsylvania conducts psycho-pharmacological experiments on prisoners under contract with the US Army.

1950-1972: Mentally disabled children at Willowbrook School in New York were deliberately infected with hepatitis in an attempt to find a vaccine.

1969: San Antonio Contraceptive Study conducted on seventy poor Hispanic women where half were given oral contraceptives and the other half a placebo without consent.

1978: Experimental Hepatitis B vaccine trials conducted on homosexual men in New York, Los Angeles, and San Francisco.

1994: President Clinton appoints Advisory Commission on Human Radiation Experiments (ACHRE) and hearing begins regularly nonconsensual exposure to radiation over past four decades by various agencies. An apology is given to the victims.

1940-current: Mind Control experimentation begins on population under MKULTRA and other pseudonyms which has continued into the current times. The Rockefeller Commission in 1975 brought release of many records regarding CIA mind control studies to light through Freedom of Information. Later that same year, The Church Committee also shed light on unethical behavior by the CIA, FBI, and the NSA.

It should be apparent to the reader that the United States government has no qualms about using the public as guinea pigs. Therefore one should have no problem accepting the claims of thousands of Americans of possible experimentation with electromagnetic weapons as true. The early CIA experiments into mind control have set the basis for continuing research and experimentation with technologies intended to exert control on an unwary population. Thus, a separate chapter has been included on MKULTRA which has a large bearing on the experimentation we are currently witnessing. The take home message from this chapter, and the entire book for that matter, is that there is inadequate legislation protecting the public from government sponsored experimentation. We have entered an era of technological advancement in electromagnetic weapons that have allowed agencies to use society as a laboratory, giving plausible denial to those performing the research. The very nature of this technology makes victims' very real complaints appear questionable as there is no tangible way to demonstrate weapons that cannot be seen. Over the past decade complaints of experimentation with electromagnetic weapons have grown exponentially and can no longer be ignored or attributed to mental illness as has been the custom of most physicians and legislators. Society has become the new laboratory, the public guinea pigs, for the technologies of control.

CHAPTER 2
MKULTRA

"For this reason God sends them a powerful delusion so that they will follow the lie."

–2Thessalonians 2:11

At the end of WWII many German physicists, medical doctors, scientists, and psychiatrists were brought to the US through secret channels without State Department approval. Much akin to the Underground Railroad that the Catholic Church provided to Nazi war criminals, the United States Government brought Nazi researchers to the United States to continue their work. Afraid of losing ground to the Germans in many scientific disciplines, these academic war criminals were allowed to escape the Nuremberg Trials in favor of academic positions in the United States. Their entry into the United States was facilitated through two OSS operations called Project Paperclip and Project 63. Over 1,000 researchers were allowed entry into the United States through these projects. Many of them were physicians guilty of mind control experiments at concentration camps such as Dachau, where the effects of mescaline and other mind altering drugs were tested on prisoners. One such physician was Dr. Kurt Platner. Another Nazi transplant, Dr. Hubertus Strughold, went on to become the director of the United States Air Force School of Aviation Medicine at Randolph AFB in San Antonio, Texas. Others close to Strughold were tried at the Nuremberg Trials; however, he amazingly avoided accusation or interrogation and has a library dedicated to him at Randolph Brooks AFB in Texas. Ironically, all of the Armed Forces research on directed-energy weapons is also done at Brooks City Base situated on the southeast side of San Antonio, Texas.

Undoubtedly, many of the doctors who began mind control research in Germany were allowed to continue that research in the United States. The OSS became the CIA and the horrors at Dachau became government funded projects with a myriad of codenames like MKULTRA, MKSEARCH, ARTICHOKE and BLUEBIRD. Similar to concentration camp victims in Nazi Germany, the American public would become the unwilling guinea pigs of most of these government funded abuses of human rights. Despite extensive shredding of documents at the order of CIA director Richard Helms, many previously classified documents pertaining to these mind control experiments were released through the Freedom of Information Act. The descriptions of certain subprojects of MKULTRA in the chapter are based on the documents released by our government and not conjecture on the part of the author. While many of the documents were heavily redacted, a definite link can be made to the complaints of continuing mind control experimentation today. Out of the 149 subprojects of MKULTRA, we will briefly delve into the ones that may have some bearing on the continued experimentation that exists today. Many believe that MKULTRA is currently ongoing under a different codename with documentation still unreleased through the FOIA.

MKULTRA was created by the CIA in 1953 and continued, according to documents, until 1972 under codename

MKSEARCH. Many of the MKSEARCH documents remain classified to date and the documents that were released are heavily redacted. Most people are familiar with MKULTRA as the LSD experiments that resulted in Frank Olson's death. Olson, a biological warfare expert, allegedly committed suicide by jumping out of a window after being given LSD in a drink as part of a CIA experiment. The drug was covertly administered by Dr. Sidney Gottlieb, Director of MKULTRA, and Olson was left under the care of Dr. Robert Lashbrook. Supposedly, as Lashbrook slept in the same hotel room, Olson leapt from the 10th story window. Later investigations have suggested that Olson may have had some help finding his way out the window. Nevertheless, Dr. Lashbrook would later testify to the Senate about the confusion regarding the CIA's files released about this incident and other MKULTRA drug programs. As stated before, the released documents are heavily redacted and somewhat confusing. The reason for this confusion, according to Lashbrook, is that separate cover files were created for each legitimate file. The cover files containing partial facts, false facts or diversionary material were the ones presented to the investigative committees while the real files remained exclusively under CIA control.

MKULTRA consisted of 149 subprojects that were all aimed at mind control. The LSD experiments were a small part of it. However, it must be noted that LSD was first synthesized by Dr. Albert Hoffman in 1943 for Sandoz, a pharmaceutical company in Switzerland. The CIA, desirous of an American source of LSD, procured a grant for the Eli Lilly Company to manufacture and provide LSD to the CIA. However, as a whole, the subprojects ranged from drug testing to behavioral studies and much, much more. The recurring theme in all of the studies was the attempt to control human emotion, human thought, and human behavior by any means available. While the CIA funding was either covert or through front companies, many of the studies found their way into peer-reviewed literature as legitimate medical studies. As I've repeatedly stated in interviews, a great majority of the MKULTRA sub projects were done at large, prestigious universities, not in the dark dungeons at Langley. Obviously, the experimental review boards at these universities, entrusted with protecting the rights of human test subjects, turned a blind eye to the abusive nature of this research. To link the early MKULTRA experiments to the continuing mind control experimentation that is going on today, we will focus on several specific subprojects. As noted earlier, there were 149 subprojects that all involved finding methods to control thought and influence behavior. These several subprojects should allow the reader to extrapolate the direction in which the research was heading. Thousands of people today are voicing complaints of subliminal control, hearing voices in their heads and being attacked with directed energy weapons. The following subprojects of MKULTRA paved the way for the experimentation we see happening today:

Subprojects 5, 25, 29, 49

All of these subprojects were conducted by Dr. Alden Sears. They involved the study of hypnosis, recall of hypnotically acquired information, hypnotic techniques and methods of hypnotizing unwilling subjects. All were labeled as "top secret." They were done under the auspices of the University of Denver and the University of Minnesota. These four subprojects ran between 1953 and 1956 with an estimated budget of 75,000 US dollars.

Subprojects 23, 45

These subprojects were contracted to Charles Geschickter from 1953 to1956 and were labeled as top secret. They were done under the auspices of the University of Richmond and the National Institute of Health. Subproject 23 involved the study of chemical agents that would modify the function of the central nervous system. Subproject 45, through the NIH involved the development of techniques to maximize physical and emotional stress in human beings.

Subproject 62

Maitland Baldwin supervised this subproject through the NIH in 1956. It involved the stimulation of monkey's brains with various radio frequencies.

Subproject 68

Directed by Dr. Ewen Cameron, this subproject was conducted in 1957 at McGill University. It studied the effects of repeated verbal signals on human behavior. Cameron published his results in the American Journal of Psychiatry in an article entitled "Psychic Driving." Psychic Driving entailed de-patterning a subject through massive amounts of electro convulsive therapy, drugs, and deprivation. Following de-patterning, the subjects were then played repetitive loops of recorded material to re-create a new personality. Many victims were left incontinent, amnesic, and unable to return to normal society. Dr. Cameron was the President of the American Psychiatric Association and was eulogized after his death as having made "outstanding contributions to the mental health of the Canadian people."

Subproject 94

This subproject was conducted through the Bio-Research Inc. Company and the Panoramic Research Company. Both companies were funded with CIA dollars. They were studying remote control behavior through brain stimulation.

Subproject 119

Dr. Saul Sells directed this project under the auspices of Texas Christian University in 1960. He was researching the techniques of controlling the human organism by remote electronic means.

The subjects in this subproject were unwitting and many were children. I have interviewed one of the childhood subjects of this subproject who is now in her fifties. She claims she is still being subjected to covert experimentation.

Subproject 138

Conducted at the University of Texas at Austin in 1961, this subproject involved the creation of biomedical sensors. Its subjects were unwilling.

Under the umbrella of MKULTRA, several researchers also investigated the use of brain implants to alter the human condition. Some of this research fell under the previously mentioned subprojects and many had overlap between subprojects. The goal was the same in all of the studies; to control human behavior through the introduction of electric shock, radio frequency or directed energy to the brain. While most readers familiar with MKULTRA may see it as a dark past in our nation's medical research, there is ample evidence that it is continuing today. Brain stimulation is one of the topics of research that began with MKULTRA and has continued in several university settings today. However, after the congressional hearings that resulted in Freedom of Information exposure of MKULTRA, the funding sources of the current research is being held closer to the vest.

The most notable physician that took part in MKULTRA brain electrode studies was Dr. Jose Delgado. Delgado, a Yale neurosurgeon, was funded by the Navy, Air Force, and the Public Health Service to research the effects of brain stimulation on epilepsy and group behavior. The emphasis here is on the "group behavior" aspect, as most of the literature released in medical journals from these studies focused on the "epilepsy" part of the research. This research included planting electrodes in the brains of both animals and humans, allowing him to control their movements and emotion. In one eleven year old boy, he was able to elicit a change in sexual identity by stimulating the superior temporal convolution of the brain. Upon stimulation, the boy would identify himself as female and express the desire to marry a male. Other doctors supplied with Delgado's implants performed their own experimentation at various universities and hospitals. Dr. Vernon Mark and Dr. Frank Ervin used Delgado's techniques to implant patients at Harvard and later at UCLA. Under Dr. Louis Jolyon West at UCLA, the plan was to use brain implants to control criminal violence in an urban setting. Both Delgado and Ervin published books detailing the use of brain implants to control behavior in a future utopian society. Delgado's book, entitled "Physical Control of the Mind: Toward a Psycho-civilized Society", should alert the reader to the exact nature of these experiments.

Another physician conducting brain electrode research was Dr. Robert Heath from the Department of Psychiatry and Neurology at Tulane University. He was an associate of Delgado, Ervin and Mark. He published several papers on the various uses of brain stimulation. His most notable study was entitled, "Septal Stimulation for the Initiation of Heterosexual Activity in a Homosexual Male." In this study, he implanted a brain electrode in a homosexual subject who was then stimulated while viewing heterosexual pornography and interacting with female prostitutes in an attempt to re-train the pleasure center of his brain to respond to women instead of men. Several other studies conducted by Dr. Heath included using brain implants to stimulate orgasms in female test subjects.

Advances in technology took the brain stimulation studies a huge step forward in the late 1960's and early 1970's. Negating the need for brain implantation, researchers now turned the exposure of the brain to external electromagnetic fields to procure similar results to brain implantation. This step would have direct implications to the complaints of mind control experimentation that we are hearing today. As it would be discovered, the human brain is very responsive to externally applied electromagnetic fields.

Two doctors in particular have done the bulk of the research using electromagnetic fields to alter human brain activity. Dr. Michael Persinger, currently at Laurentian University in Canada, has studied the ability of magnetic fields to create false memories and alter consciousness for many years. Some of his research has been funded by the Department of the Navy and he sits on the Board of the False Memory Syndrome Foundation (FMSF). The FMSF has maintained a hostile stance against the reality of multiple personality disorder. Indeed, multiple personality disorder is the technique used in MKULTRA to create Manchurian Candidates. According to the FMSF, multiple personality disorder, if it exists, is created by the therapist in a manner akin to cult brain washing. It must be noted that many other members of the FMSF have also been involved in MKULTRA subprojects. It is my opinion, as should be evident to the reader that the goal of the FMSF is to spread misinformation and divert attention away from the current research on mind control.

A brief review of Dr. Persinger's research will bring up titles such as "Psychophysiological Effects of Extremely Low Frequency Electromagnetic Fields, Classical Psychophysics and ELF Magnetic Field Detection, Possible Learned Detection of Exogenous Brain Frequency Electromagnetic Fields, and Enhancement of Temporal Lobe-Related Experiences During Brief Exposure to Milligauss Intensity Extremely Low Frequency Magnetic Fields." Dr. Persinger is accredited with developing the "God Helmet" which, when placed on a subject's head, uses microwave energy to stimulate the temporal lobes of the brain. The subject will then have spiritual experiences akin to being in the presence of a supreme being or having alien contact.

In the article, "On the Possibility of directly Accessing Every Human Brain by Electromagnetic Induction of Fundamental Algorithms," he mentioned the potential for the capability of directly influencing the major portion of the approximately six billion brains of the human species. He goes on to mention that this could be accomplished by generating neural information within a physical medium within which all members of the species could be immersed. Dr. Persinger claims that, with the exception of a small amount of Naval funding, all of his work has been funded by his private practice. Many find this unbelievable with what we know about the twisted trails of funding provided to other researchers through intelligence agency front companies. In the book "Remote Viewers" by Jim Schnabel, Dr. Persinger is mentioned as being included in a still classified project called "Sleeping Beauty." This Defense Intelligence Agency funded project focuses on the ability of electromagnetic fields to create false memories and altered states of consciousness.

Dr. William Ross Adey has done work similar to Dr. Persinger's research involving electromagnetic fields. Most of Dr. Adey's research has been done at UCLA under contract from the United States Air Force and United States Navy. He edited a publication for the MIT Neurosciences Research Program entitled "Brain Interaction with Weak Electronic and Magnetic Fields." It must be noted that Dr. Adey has functioned as a consultant for NASA, the Veterans Administration, the Department of Energy and the Medical Hazards of Microwave Exposure, and the US/USSR Exchange Program. In the 1980's Doctor Adey demonstrated how a 147 MHz field with a power band of .8mw per square centimeter caused an efflux of calcium ions from the irradiated brain tissue. The response occurred when the 147 MHz carrier frequency was modulated at 6-20 Hz, an ELF range of frequency.

Many of the government funded research projects into various parapsychological phenomenons were piggybacked on to the MKULTRA program. While none of the subproject descriptions from the FOIA releases specifically mention the inclusion of ESP or PSI studies, it is known that funding was intertwined and that many of the MKULTRA researched dabbled in such studies. Of interest, the remote viewing studies of the 1960's and 1970's have a direct relation to both MKULTRA and current, ongoing experimentation.

Lastly, this chapter on MKULTRA is not meant to be a complete description of the program. Many great books have been written that go into great detail about each subproject of MKULTRA. It is the author's intent to introduce those subprojects that have a direct bearing on the complaints of mind control experimentation still ongoing today. MKULTRA set a precedent for the government's desire to learn how to control the human mind and alter human behavior through that control. It also demonstrates further a willingness on the part of the government to covertly experiment on an unwitting public. I believe the first two chapters of this book should impress upon the reader that the United States Government has and will continue to use the unwitting public as guinea pigs for this type of experimentation.

CHAPTER 3

Remote Influencing

"For by thy sorceries were all nations deceived."

–Revelations 18:23

The Soviet Union was the first to recognize and research a very unique phenomenon among human beings called remote viewing or remote influencing. At first, though it only existed in a handful of individuals with innate ability, it is now thought to be a capability of most human beings with appropriate training. Remote influencing is the ability of an individual to view and interact with another individual in a remote location without physically connecting to that location. By definition, physically connecting would include traveling to that location or connecting via any form of synthetic communication technology. Remote viewing, similar to remote influencing, is the ability to see a remote location without physically traveling to that location. The Soviet Union was much more interested in remote influencing than the pure surveillance method of remote viewing. As information about Soviet research found its way outside the iron curtain, the United States quickly found itself pursuing similar avenues of research. Stories of Soviet psychic research prompted the 1972 Defense Intelligence Agency report titled "Controlled Offensive Behavior – USSR." The report alluded to the possibility of their research to enable them to know contents of United States classified documents, positions of troops, locations of military installations, and to modify the thoughts of personnel and cause death remotely via telepathy. The release of this report prompted the race for similar research in the United States by almost every branch of the DoD as well as our intelligence agencies.

In the Soviet Union two scientists in particular are noted to have done the majority of the research into remote influencing. Dr. Leonid Vasiliev, chairman of the psychology department at the University of Leningrad, headed up a very vigorous parapsychology research center. He is quoted as stating that, "the discovery of the energy underlying ESP will be equivalent to the discovery of atomic energy." Vasiliev's research was guided by the electromagnetic hypothesis of telepathy put forth by neuropsychiatrist Hans Berger. Berger's pursuit of a measurable carrier of telepathy led to his discovery of the electrical potential of the brain we refer to as the EEG. Vasiliev's research continued until his death in 1966. A revised English translation of his work was published in 1976 under the title "Experiments in Distant Influence." He was able to remotely influence changes in subjects such as motor acts, visual images, sleepiness, wakefulness and changes in electro-dermal activity. His results were positive despite attempts at shielding the electromagnetic waves with iron, lead, and Faraday chamber screening material.

The other Soviet researcher who spent much of his time studying telepathy and remote influencing was Professor I.M. Kogan. An electrical engineer, Kogan postulated that PSI was merely an extremely low frequency radio system built into human brains. Kogan's studies, as well as more modern studies, would demonstrate that electromagnetic shielding attempts would not successfully stop the phenomenon of remote viewing and remote influence. This perpetuated the ELF wave theory and the mode of delivery of telepathic phenomena. Electromagnetic shielding is known to have little attenuation of ELF waves as they travel great distances. Opponents of the ELF wave theory argue that the bit of data transfer using ELF waves would not be great enough to communicate full sentences in a reasonable amount of time. However, as written in the chapter on MKULTRA, Dr. Michael Persinger's research focused heavily on ELF wave effects on the human brain.

Not to be left out of the race, the United States began its own research into remote viewing. The two names most recognized as having done most, if not at all, of the research in remote viewing are Dr. Harold Puthoff and Dr. Russel Targ. In 1972 the Office of Technical Services, under directorship of Dr. Sydney Gottlieb, an MKULTRA contractor, awarded Dr. Puthoff his remote viewing funding. Code named Stargate and Grill Flame, the operations were not part of MKULTRA but were very close cousins to it both in funding and type of research. 20 million dollars would be spent on remote viewing studies that were continued into the 1990's. The majority of the finding came from the CIA and the DoD with the bulk of the research being done at Ft. Meade and Stanford Research Institute.

One particular incident catapulted the CIA into the parapsychological research business. In the early 1970's President Nixon claimed that he and several others of his staff had experienced "inappropriate times of crying" after a visit to the Soviet Union. It wasn't long after that confession that the CIA put 20,000 dollars in Dr. Puthoff's hands at Stanford Research Institute's Menlo Park Research Center. Research and development into remote influencing began with such notable characters as Ingo Swann, Uri Gellar, Pat Price and a handful of military recruits. The viewers were tasked with coordinates of known locations and asked to draw or describe what they viewed in a trancelike state from the research center. No clues were given and most of the time the research assistants were not even allowed to know what actually existed at the chosen coordinates. The resulting descriptions and drawings of the locations being tasked were eerily accurate and caught serious attention from the CIA and NSA. With the Soviet Union much further ahead in this type of research, could remote viewing be an almost impossible security breach to combat? Soon INSCOM was also researching remote viewing with General Albert Stubblebine at the helm. A "New-Ager" seeking alternative paranormal projects, Stubblebine's projects were made popular in the motion picture "Men Who Stare at Goats."

Despite all of the research and its successes, a serious question still kept arising. What is the mechanism behind remote viewing and remote influencing? The various theories put forth attempting to explain the mode of transmission of data in remote viewing have included ELF waves, tachyons, RF, and quantum theory. Puthoff and Targ set out to determine the mechanism by placing remote viewers in anechoic chambers during their experiments. The chambers were checked for any electronic bugging devices and secured from any chance of the viewer receiving outside information. The remote viewers were still able to accurately describe their assigned coordinates without any noticeable impairment. The only electromagnetic waves known to penetrate anechoic chambers are ELF waves. Were the Russians correct in their ELF wave hypothesis for the transmission of telepathic events? In an attempt to answer this question, Puthoff and Targ began measuring natural magnetic field fluctuations in the area by connecting an ELF signal amplifier to trees outside their office. Trees are nature's best ELF wave antennas. If remote viewing is dependent on ELF waves, then severe fluctuations in the magnetosphere should interfere with remote viewing. According to Puthoff and Targ, even large geomagnetic fluctuations did not impede successful remote viewing. To this day Puthoff and Targ disagree with the ELF wave theory and telepathic transmission. During this phase of the research attention was also focused on the brains of the viewers. They were given numerous psychological tests, neurological exams and electro encephalograms. Magnetic encephalographs were performed at Los Alamos Laboratory to measure deep brain waves which led investigators to suspect temporal lobe involvement in telepathic functioning. Amazingly, Dr. Persinger's work, which has continued into the present, involves bombarding the temporal lobes of the brain with various forms of electromagnetic energy.

While much of this research seems to border on the fringe of science fiction, it has continued in recent times. Remote viewing is still being actively studied by several privately funded groups made up of former Stargate test subjects. Several are known to hire out their services. In addition, many of Vasiliev's remote influencing experiments have been successfully replicated by current researchers. Through the support of the Mind Science Foundation, an organization of which I am a member, Vasiliev's experiments were replicated by William G. Braud and associates. Specifically, the experiments involving remotely influencing a subject's skin resistance responses were done. The experiments were not carried out using special subjects with known telepathic ability as they were under Vasiliev's direction in the Soviet Union. Subjects were selected randomly from the community. One subject was selected as an influencer and one subject was selected to be the receiver. The influencer was instructed to telepathically attempt to alter the receiver's physiology from 20km away, while the receiver was connected to electronic sensors to measure skin resistance. More statistically significant in skin electro dermal activity occurred with remote activation than without. These studies are viewed as successful replications of distal mental suggestion.

Taken at face value, the early research into remote viewing would appear to be unrelated to any of the issues regarding current covert experimentation. However, several things regarding remote viewing place its early research into question. This is not a question about legitimacy or methods of research. We know quite a bit about the Stargate studies through books written by its subjects and investigators. Puthoff and Targ have both published many of their declassified findings and have appeared on public radio stations. It is my opinion that the findings Puthoff and Targ found to be positive were not necessarily the same findings the CIA was gleaning from their studies. Puthoff and Targ were mainly looking to prove that an innate human telepathic ability does exist and can be scientifically quantified and used in a positive manner. The CIA was more interested in the byproducts of their research. First, the initial funding came from the Office of Technical Services under the directorship of Dr. Sydney Gottlieb, an MKULTRA subcontractor. Secondly, in addition to establishing that remote viewing is possible, it was also discovered that part of the brain plays a role in its function. Thirdly, through the use of anechoic chambers, it was found that ELF waves may indeed be the mode of transmission of projected thought. Ironically, while Puthoff and Targ continued to disagree with the ELF wave hypothesis, continuing research focused on ELF wave effects on the human brain and not the phenomenon of remote viewing. Furthermore, the temporal lobes of the human brain became the targets of continued research using various forms of electromagnetic energy. This almost certainly ushered in the next phase of research known as remote neural monitoring and probably was the impetus for the development of The High Frequency Active Auroral Research Program. HAARP is the multi-billion dollar ELF wave generator nestled in the woods of Alaska and relatively closed to public viewing. Obviously the CIA took the ELF wave hypothesis much more seriously than some of the researchers experimenting with remote viewing.

CHAPTER 4
Remote Neural Monitoring

"For my thoughts are not your thoughts,
neither are your ways my ways."

–Isaiah 55:8

The MKULTRA research and the remote viewing research alluded scientists to not only what effects they wanted, but what part of the brain to focus on to get those effects. While a few scientists disagreed with the ELF wave hypothesis, the majority of the research both in the United States and the Soviet Union continued to focus on the effects of ELF waves on the brain. However, one problem still remained. Many of the victims of MKULTRA had been unwitting subjects who had been lied to and coerced into unethical experimentation. The technologic limitations at the time had necessitated sequestering victims into hospitals where they could be drugged and subjected to electro-convulsive therapy using electrodes placed on the scalp. Physiologic monitoring of the EEG and other vital signs also required sensors placed on the subject. In addition, things had become a little hot for the MKULTRA researchers by the early 1970's. Victims' complaints had prompted congressional hearings and the unethical experimentation conducted by the CIA on unwitting subjects began to be exposed. With Senator Ted

Kennedy at the helm, CIA documents that survived the shredding machine painted a picture of bizarre unethical experimentation, mostly done through front companies. Had the CIA not sequestered victims in research centers for experimentation and left a paper trail, there may have never been disclosure in congressional hearings. The public was outraged at the abuse. The congress was dismayed. The CIA began looking for other ways to continue their mind control research with greater plausible deniability and less chance of getting caught with their pants down. The era of remote neural monitoring had begun.

The Advanced Research Projects Agency awarded a contract for $338,000 to the Stanford Research Institute (CSRI) on February 9, 1972. The program director was Dr. George Lawrence and the contract was granted to Dr. Lawrence Pinneo to determine the feasibility of bio-cybernetic communication. More specifically, Dr. Pinneo was researching the feasibility of designing a communication link between man and computer using electrical activity of the brain during verbal thinking. The hypothesis was that the electrical activity of the brain during thought may be similar to the electrical activity of the brain during overt speech. The EEGs of the subjects were measured using scalp electrodes over the frontal-temporal lobes. "The research was predicated on the assumption that thought is nothing more than covert speech." Subjects were shown picture cards of the words they were to think about as their EEGs were recorded. The research concluded that the EEG reveals similar responses during silent reading to that during overt speech and that these responses may be classified correctly by a computer with a high degree of accuracy.

Pinneo's study also focused on identifying the EEG patterns of homonyms. Homonyms are words like "write" and "right" which are pronounced the same, but have different meanings.

EEG patterns were similar when subjects thought the single word "write" or "right." However, if the subjects thought of the word in the context of a phrase, the EEG was capable of discriminating similarly articulated words. Electrodes were placed at various sites on the scalp; however, temporal lobe electrodes demonstrated the most statistically significant accuracy. To the contrary, electrodes placed over the occipital or parietal areas of the brain had a no better than chance correlation.

One must remember that Dr. Pinneo's research was conducted in 1972 with relatively crude technology for measuring the EEG. Despite technological shortcomings, he was still able to construct an EEG dictionary of certain words that were only thought by the subjects. Similar to the remote viewing studies, he determined that the temporal lobes of the brain were the most valuable in measuring the EEG representation of thought. In addition, he observed parameters that would increase the accuracy of the EEG corresponding to the covertly thought word or phrase. These parameters included training the subject in the operating system and using temporal training for covert responses, giving the subject set responses to think about and using words or phrases that are meaningful to the subject. Overall, Dr. Pinneo's research in 1972 determined that a bio-cybernetic communication system was feasible which would allow a computer to interpret human thought based on the EEG. Not surprisingly, included in his references of his study are studies performed by Dr. W. R. Adey, a MKULTRA subcontractor.

The research that followed focused on remotely sensing the small, electrical potentials generated by the brain. Remotely detecting the EEG would negate the need for scalp electrodes and alleviate the requirement for informal consent on the subjects. One researcher, Robert G. Malech, researched remotely monitoring and altering brain waves which culminated in the filing U.S. Patent number 3951134 in 1974. His apparatus involved transmitting a base signal and a first signal to the brain of a monitored subject. The brain of the subject would then transmit a second signal back to a receiver in response to the two incoming signals. Essentially, the two incoming signals would entrain with the brain's inherent electrical frequency and or interference waveform would be returned to a receiver. The interference waveform could then be demodulated, amplified and displayed visually before being routed to a computer. According to Malech, the demodulated waveform would be used to produce a compensating signal which could be transmitted back to the brain. The compensating signal could be artificially attempted to entrain the normal brain activity and produce a desired change in the subjects' brain. In Malech's description of the apparatus he specifically mentioned its value in monitoring a conscious subject without his awareness. His patent was published in 1976 and his apparatus was comprised of components commonly employed in radar systems at the same time.

Coincidentally, another discovery relating to radar installations was the Frey effect or microwave hearing, which will be covered later.

Malech's concluding paragraph in the published patent stated: "Persons in critical positions such as drivers and pilots can be continuously monitored with provisions for activation of an emergency device in the event of human failure. Seizures, sleepiness and dreaming can be detected. Bodily functions such as pulse rate, heartbeat regularity and others can also be monitored and occurrences of hallucinations can be detected. The system also permits medical diagnoses of patients inaccessible to physicians from remote stations."

It must be remembered that Malech's apparatus was theorized in 1976 with vastly inferior technology compared to today.

Advances in computational speed and monitoring technology have taken Dr. Pinneo's EEG dictionary and Malech's remote EEG monitoring apparatus further than even they had dreamed. Using these basic concepts, more modern research has focused on converting the received electromagnetic waveforms back into audible thought that can be monitored and recorded. Essentially, mind reading has come of age and has been in use among intelligence agencies for a number of years now. In addition to monitoring a subject's thoughts, researchers have also capitalized on Malech's earlier discovered EEG entrainment techniques. Once a dictionary of EEG waveforms corresponding to various emotional states was created, it became relatively easy to cause a normal subject's brain to entrain the desired waveform to produce a desired emotional state. One would assume that using the same technique, the visual and auditory cortices of the brain could be entrained to stimulate visual and auditory hallucinations respectively. This would result in what subjects would perceive as realistic appearing holograms or sounds that cannot be attributed to a realistic source in their surroundings. Indeed, thousands of people across the United States are voicing complaints of just this phenomenon.

While this may be sounding a bit like science fiction at this point, if the reader places the current research into context with the earlier MKULTRA studies, the desired goals seem clear. The agencies behind the research were avidly looking for methods to hear thoughts in real-time for the purposes of covert communication, lie detection and behavioral modification. Not to be left out of the "mind-race," the various armed focuses have funded their own independent research into remote neural monitoring. The Army refers to the technology of decoding thought into a real-time audible signal as "synthetic telepathy." A team of University of California at Irvine researchers has been

awarded a 4 million dollar grant to research and develop a method
for soldiers in the field to communicate telepathically. This will
be accomplished through a brain computer interface in which
one soldier's EEG will be remotely sensed and decoded, then
transmitted to another's brain as an audible signal or thought.
Researchers admit that there will be a steep learning curve as
soldiers train themselves to communicate with each other using
thoughts alone and not spoken words. The grant money, your tax
dollars, comes from the United States Department of Defense's
Multidisciplinary University Research Initiative Program. This
program supports research involving more than one science and
engineering discipline. At face value, the Army's admission of
this undertaking appears innocent enough and could quite possibly
have important national security implications. However, there is
a more alarming admission if one reads between the lines. Their
current research is focusing on interactive synthetic telepathy
between multiple war fighters in the field. It is the opinion of the
author that this is an admission that the technology has already
been perfected in a bi-directional manner between a targeted
subject and a communication system. This has particular
relevance when one takes into consideration the increasing
number of people complaining of hearing voices in their heads.
Knowing the history of covert experimentation in this country,
is it possible that the public has been used as unwitting guinea
pigs in researching this technology? An argument can easily be
made that this is the case.

More current research into remote neural monitoring has
involved decoding the action potentials arising in the speech
cortex that sends signals to the muscles of speech. Everyone has
heard of the old adage, "don't speak without thinking." As it turns
out, this is impossible. Thoughts are the precursors to speech and
this establishes the basis of remote neural monitoring, synthetic

telepathy and thought controlled devices. Many researchers have focused on sensing the evoked potentials originating in the speech cortex and using the signal to control various devices by thought alone. In order to achieve this, one must elucidate the bio-mechanics of speech and hearing as it pertains to the electromagnetic potentials generated in both the auditory and speech centers of the brain. Once again, the temporal lobes of the human brain have proven to be the area most involved in speech and hearing. In 1999, researchers at Albert Einstein College of Medicine published a paper in the International Journal of Neurophysiology in which they described recording field potentials directly from the auditory complex. Their study was most interested in determining voice onset time (VOT), the time interval between consonant onset and the onset of vocal cord vibration. Establishing the time delay between the brain signaling the vocal cords and the vocal cords actually responding to generate speech is important. It allows one to know when and for what duration a signal will be present to be remotely sensed and electro-mechanically converted to a form that will activate a device. Indeed, the research has paid off. We now have digital voice generators and robotic limbs that may be controlled by thought originating from the speech centers of the brain. While this technology may prove to be invaluable to the handicapped, decoding thought may have grave consequences on society as it is used in a more covert fashion.

Thousands of people across the United States have already been complaining of being victimized by remote neural monitoring. It remains to be seen if this has been part of the experimental phase of this technology or if the technology has fallen into criminal hands. Many of the victims have been accused of being delusional. However, delusional disorder in the United States has a .03% incidence in the general population and the numbers of similarities of the complaints lends itself more to the likelihood of experimentation. Nonetheless, this very intrusive technology should prove difficult to pitch to the general public already fearful of any further loss of privacy. Maybe not! Many of the press releases are focusing on allowing the handicapped to use thought controlled devices to make their lives easier. Furthermore, at the 2009 American International Toy Fair, two children's toys were on displays that harness the EEG to move a ball around using thought. Mattel's Mindflex and Uncle Milton's Force Trainer use wireless headsets that measure alpha and beta waves which in turn trigger fans that move a foam ball up, down or sideways. The toys retail for $129.99 and $79.99 respectively. What could be more innocent and non-threatening than children's toys? Make no mistake; this is an intentional attempt at mainstreaming a form of technology that will have grave consequences on society. If you have any doubt, ask any one of the victims of this research that have lost their careers and families after being diagnosed as delusional, only to see the technology they were told did not exist appear at Toys R Us!

CHAPTER 5

Auditory Harassment

"Dear Friends, do not believe every spirit, but test the spirits
to see whether they are from God because many false prophets
have gone out into the world."

–1 John 4:1

One of the hallmark symptoms that distinguish between the mentally normal and the mentally ill is the presence of voices in the head. It is described as one of the symptoms of delusional disorder, psychosis, schizoaffective disorder and schizophrenia. Referred to as auditory hallucinations, their presence in a myriad of psychiatric disorders has been the fodder of countless journal articles and psychiatric test books. For some time now, one debate has been taking place in the psychiatric community as to when auditory hallucinations constitute mental illness. Traditionally anyone hearing voices that no one else can hear have been presumed to be mentally ill. A more moderate approach ascertains the context during which auditory hallucinations are heard before passing judgment. For instance, it's perfectly acceptable to tell others that God told you to start going to church more regularly. God instructing you to kill your neighbors, however, is generally seen as mental illness. An even more liberal approach to auditory hallucinations holds the belief that hearing voices is acceptable in the absence of personal or socially destructive behavior. Moreover, the Hearing Voices Movement, an organization started by Marius Romme from The Netherlands, has advocated treating AH with successful coping techniques learned from other voice hearers. To date, their techniques have not generally been incorporated into common psychiatric practice; the reason being, psychiatry has increasingly become a mechanism of control and discipline rather than a medical art. There will be more regarding this statement in a later chapter.

An exhaustive search through psychiatric journals regarding AH will turn up some very interesting facts. Most of the studies done regarding AH are focused on patients diagnosed with schizophrenia. Schizophrenia occurs rarely in males and females but differs in the peak age of onset between the sexes. Men usually develop schizophrenia between the ages of 20-28 years, while women may be diagnosed between the ages of 26-32 years. This is an important fact to remember for later in this text. Also, the geographic distribution of schizophrenia varies wildly. However, people living in urban areas seem to be more likely to be diagnosed. Descriptions of the voices they hear include single voices and groups of voices. Schizophrenics often describe the voices as persecutory in nature, criticizing their behavior or appearance. More often, the voices are described as garbled and unintelligible akin to many muffled voices in a subway. The etiology of schizophrenia in unknown; however, excess dopamine is thought to play a role. Drugs that limit dopamine production or block dopamine receptors are the mainstay of treatment. It is thought that schizophrenia affects .4% - .6% of the population. A common belief among those diagnosed with schizophrenia is that the voices and thoughts are being inserted into their heads from an external source.

Two startling facts are apparent when one reviews the literature on schizophrenia and its associated auditory hallucinations. The same holds true for AH secondary to psychosis (non-schizophrenic) and delusional disorder. Firstly, few of the studies ever mention the specific dialogue attributed to "the voices." They are often described as pleasant, persecutory or religious in nature without any specificity to the content of the dialogue. It is almost as if it is pre-assumed that hearing voices at all, regardless of their content, is a symptom of mental illness. Regarding schizophrenia, the use of white noise or static over a radio or television is often described as a coping mechanism to drown out "the voices." This is an important description that will be further discussed later in this chapter. Secondly, there is absolutely no mention in any of the psychiatric studies of the possibility that technology exists to place voices in one's head. One would assume that, with psychiatrists at the helm of the early mind control studies, there would be at least a suggestion that we now have the technology to reproduce the symptoms of schizophrenia. Thousands of people are currently voicing just that complaint. Individuals, many of them professionals with no history of mental illness, are complaining of hearing voices. The number of these complaints far exceeds published percentages of schizophrenia and delusional disorder as a percentage of the total population. It is my opinion that many of the people complaining of auditory harassment may indeed be victims of harassment technology and not a mental disease. I find it highly unlikely that large groups of schizophrenics voicing similar complaints would be corresponding with each other over the internet looking for answers to their dilemma. However, that is exactly what is happening! So, does the technology exist to place voices in one's head or surroundings that only they can hear, mimicking the symptoms of mental illness? The literature indeed does illustrate the fact that such technology exists. Moreover, research has been underway for quite some time with the goal of placing communications in a person's head. Admittedly, some of the research has had noble expectations; however, most of it has been weapons based research with less than noble expectations. So, why does the psychiatric community refuse to consider technologic harassment as an etiology of auditory hallucinations in persons usually required to see them? We will ponder the answer to that question in a later chapter dedicated in its entirety to the psychiatric profession. For now, we'll continue with the technologic causes of what may appear to be auditory hallucinations.

Dr. G. Patrick Flanagan was born in 1944 in Oklahoma and was known as somewhat of a child prodigy in scientific endeavors. At the age of 12 years old he invented a missile detection system that quickly got the attention of the DoD. At age 14 he invented a device called the Neurophone that allowed sound to be transmitted to the brain through the skin. The year was 1958 and the device worked despite the crude technology of the day. As technology advanced, production of the Neurophone continued with modern circuit boards and digital processing into the current model that is available today. The Neurophone does have the ability to place voices in the head that only the user can hear. How it works has only recently been elucidated. Apparently, humans do have the ability to detect ultrasonic sound through tissues in the body. In 1991 Martin Lenhardt, at the University of Virginia, discovered that humans can perceive ultrasonic sound through an inner ear organ called the saccule. The saccule is actually an organ used for balance; however, when stimulated with ultrasonic sound it sends neural signals to the part of the brain used for sound. It has been postulated that our ability to hear the pops and clicks of dolphins while scuba diving is perceived through the saccule. Capitalizing on this phenomenon, the Neurophone utilizes two electrodes that may be placed anywhere on the body. The circuitry of the device has been engineered to provide a means for ultrasonic waves to be passed through the tissue to the saccule. The result is sound that "can be clearly heard as if it were coming from inside the brain." The current model of the Neurophone has audio inputs that allow for music or meditation aids to be played through the electrodes and into the brain.

Obviously, schizophrenics do not hear voices as a result of electrodes placed on their body that transmit ultrasonic sound. The Neurophone merely sets that precedent for obvious attempts to place audio in a person's head. Further research took the required steps to get the same results without the need for electrodes. Some researchers took the path of finding ways to place silent, subliminal messages into the brain while others focused on the audible component as a weapon and tool for harassment. The discoveries of Allan Frey paved the way for the latter. Research done on subliminal messaging is equally important and will be discussed later. For the most part, subliminal signals are non-audible and do not directly constitute auditory harassment.

In 1960, while working at General Electrics Advanced Electronics Center at Cornell University, Frey discovered that he could "hear" radar. The discovery came after a radar technician told him that he could hear the radar at one particular site where he worked. After some research, Frey ascertained that the sound, heard in the brain, was secondary to the interaction of electromagnetic radiation and brain cells and was not heard through normal hearing mechanisms. It was termed the "Frey Effect" and set the basis for many ongoing studies into intracranial communication. Frey went on to study the non-thermal effects of microwaves and came to some very interesting conclusions.

Microwaves belong to a part of the electromagnetic spectrum which are included in radar, microwave ovens and all cell phones. Their non-thermal effects can be as equally detrimental as their thermal effects, as witnessed every day in microwave ovens. Frey targeted various organ systems with microwaves and was able to reproduce detrimental effects, including heart arrhythmias, and sudden death. Modulated microwave frequencies, those carrying a second embedded frequency, were found to be the most damaging. In 1975, Frey reported that microwave energy pulsed at certain modulations could breach the blood-brain behavior and induce neurologic changes. The DoD took a keen interest in Frey's research. They were intrigued not only with the use of microwave as a directed energy weapon, but as a carrier signal for communications to be placed directly in the brain. This is now called "microwave auditory effect" and has been extensively researched by the government and private institutions. Finally, the need for electrodes, as with the Neurophone, was a thing of the past.

The microwave auditory effect (MAE) has been extensively studied, amazingly, in the psychological community. Dr. Joseph Sharp and Mark Grove were the first to capitalize on the effect while doing research for the Advanced Research Projects Agency at Walter Reed Army Institute of Research. In 1973 they were able to develop receiver-less, wireless technology for communication and were able to transmit single syllable words into their own heads. In 1975 Dr. Jon Justensen, Laboratories of Experimental Neuropsychology VA Hospital Kansas City, MO, summarized and verified Dr. Sharp's findings in an article entitled "Microwaves and Behavior." It was published in The American Psychologist (Volume 30, March 1975, Number 3.) Sharp and Grove used pulsed modulated microwave energy to transmit single syllables into the head. They were reluctant to attempt combinations of words for fear they would surpass safe exposure limits of microwave energy and induce detrimental thermal effects. Continued research has elucidated the most likely mechanism for the microwave auditory effect.

The proposed mechanism is through thermo-elastic expansion of tissues in the head that transmit an acoustic pressure wave to the cochlea. Once the cochlear receptors are stimulated, the sound is actually perceived through the same processes as for normal hearing. In 2003, published in the Journal Bio-electromagnetics, JA Elder and CK Chou found that the auditory response is dependent on the energy in a single pulse and not on the average power density. They also found that perception of the sound is somewhat dependent on head dimensions. "Effective radiofrequencies range from 2.4 to 10,000 MHz, but an individual's ability to hear RF induced sound is dependent upon high frequency acoustic hearing in the KHz range above about 5 KHz." Also, according to Elder and Chou, hearing an RF induced sound at exposure levels many orders of a magnitude greater than the hearing threshold level is considered to be a biological effect without an accompanying health effect. However it does not appear that they took psychiatric effects into account as health effects. Many people worldwide appear to be victims of nonconsensual experimentation regarding this technology. The ultimate result of this covert experimentation is usually a psychiatric diagnosis of delusional disorder. Despite attempts by the psychiatric community to de-stigmatize mental illness, this diagnosis is usually damning to an individual's social and occupational wellbeing. Many of these victims are living a Hitchcock-type existence, knowing they are sane in a world turned insane.

Another researcher who has done extensive research on the microwave auditory effect is James Lin. Lin is a professor and electrical engineer at the University of Illinois-Chicago and is a fellow of the IEEE. He has served as a chair on the URSI Commission on Electromagnetics in Biology and Medicine as well as the IEEE Committee on Man and Radiation. He began publishing on the microwave auditory effect in the late 1970's and has authored several books on the effects of the electromagnetic spectrum on human biology. In his Advances in Electromagnetic Fields in Living Systems he states: "Widespread applications of RF and microwave energy are found in RF article identification and surveillance, on-body sensing and interrogation, novel active and passive security and detection technology and proposed digital living network applications." Lin concurred with Elder and Chou regarding thermo-elastic expansion being the mechanism behind the microwave auditory effect in an article published in Health Physics in 2007 entitled, "Hearing of microwave pulses by humans and animals: effects, mechanism, and thresholds."

In 1996 Alfred M. Ackerman proposed another method to pass audio signals through various media such as gases, liquids, and solids. While he did not specifically mention the human head in his patent application, I believe the method would allow for audio signals to be passed through the skull. Working for Martin Marietta Energy Systems Inc. and funded by a contract from the Department of Energy, Ackerman devised a method to convert audio signals to electronic signals in the ultrasonic frequency range. The ultrasonic signals could then be converted to acoustical pressure waves that would transmit across a carrier medium such as liquids or solids. The acoustic waves could then be reconverted back to audio signals. This involves modulating the human voice audio signal on an ultrasonic carrier frequency that would also be carried across a medium with an acoustic wave. Once the carrier signal has passed through the liquid/solid medium, it can be demodulated leaving only the audio signal intact. Thus, the system can be used for communication without the use of traditional radio frequencies. In his patent, Ackerman mentions that value of this method for communications where a "high degree of security" is required. Covert radio frequency communication requires scrambling the signal or trunking between frequencies to avoid interception. Furthermore, the mere presence of radio signals could be detected and cause problems for any RF based covert communications. By using ultrasonic signals converted to acoustic waves, the communication system would be impervious to traditional RF detection systems. In his patent he states, "by way of example and not limitation, the disclosed invention is useful in a variety of applications including undercover operations, industrial applications, and many commercial uses in various media." In other words, this technology may be useful for surveillance, harassment, and corporate espionage. This method of sound propagation could explain the harassing audio many people are subjected to that is described as sound that bombards them through vibrations in the home.

Not to be outdone by the private sector, the DoD became keenly interested in the microwave auditory effect. As with most new discoveries, the government eventually finds a way to weaponize most novel technology. The microwave auditory effect was no different. Furthermore, all branches of the military began researching microwave technology as it pertains to both physical and psychological weapons. Termed "non-lethal weapons," this class includes microwaves as well as other forms of directed energy that will be discussed later. The microwave auditory effect is specifically mentioned in the Army's Addendum to the Non-Lethal Technologies Worldwide "Bio-Effects of Selected Non-Lethal Weapons" released through the Freedom of Information Act. This document, written in 1998, mentions the value of the microwave auditory effect communicating with a hostage without his captives hearing. Furthermore, it mentions its usefulness in providing a disruptive condition in a person unaware of the technology. "Not only might it be disruptive to the sense of hearing, it could be psychologically devastating if one suddenly heard voices within one's head." Moreover, microphones placed next to the person experiencing the "voices" cannot pick up the sound. The most troubling comment in the document states that, "humans have been subjected to this phenomenon for many years."

Indeed, in a Newsweek article from Aug 22, 1964 and in an article from Defense Electronics, July 1993 it was stated that the FBI enlisted the help of a Russian scientist named Igor Smirnov. Smirnov had been researching the ability to phone subliminal messages in the head for many years. During the Branch Davidian siege in Waco, Texas, the FBI met with Smirnov in Arlington, Virginia to request the use of his technology to end the siege. Their plan was to pipe the voice of God into the head of David Koresh in order to convince him to turn himself in to the authorities. According to people who attended the meeting with the FBI, Smirnov had bought only entry level equipment that was not compatible with FBI computers. To our knowledge, Smirnov's acoustic mind control technology was not used at the siege in Waco for that reason. Of note, Smirnov did most of his research at Moscow's Institute of Psycho-Correction and marketed his technology to the West through a Canadian Company called Psychotechnology Research Institute. Seeking US partners, PRI went to SRS Technologies, now part of Man Tech International Corporation. Interestingly, Man Tech is based in my hometown of San Antonio, Texas.

Weaponized versions of the microwave auditory effect and

acoustic wave technology include the MEDUSA weapon and the S-QUAD (silent sound spread spectrum) respectively. The MEDUSA weapon (mob excess deterrent using silent audio) is the brain child of Dr. Lev Sadovnik. The initial research was funded by the Navy from 11/19/2003 – 5/19/2004 under contract number M67854-04-C-1012. The Navy was interested in using the MAE as remote personnel Incapacitation system by inducing distressing sounds into the human head. The research only made it through phase I at the Navy's Small Business Innovation Research System. Dr. Sadovnik has since continued working on the MEDUSA project through the Sierra Nevada Corporation. The S-QUAD was developed by Dr. Oliver Lowery and is described in US patent #5, 159, 703 as a silent subliminal presentation system. In the patent abstract, the device is described as a system in which non aural carriers, in the very low or very high frequency range may be modulated with the desired intelligence and propagated into the brain. Silent Sounds, Inc. recently claimed that they now have the ability to analyze the human EEG, replicate it or store it, and transmit a modified EEG wave form into an intended target. Specifically emotional subsets may be stored, like an emotion dictionary, and entrained into a target that will display the desired emotion or behavior. Edward Tilton, the president of Silent Sounds, Inc. stated in a letter dated 13 December, 1996 that all schematics of the system have been classified by the US Government. Silent Sound Technology was allegedly used in the first Gulf War to subliminally induce Iraqi soldiers to surrender according to two news briefs from ITV News Bureau LTD. (London). According to the new briefs, one of the soldiers involved was quoted as stating, "They were surrendering in droves, almost too fast for us to keep up with......"

An entire book could easily be written on the research and

development of technologies meant to subliminally control the human mind or place perceived auditory hallucinations in the head. I have attempted to present some of the high points of this research to demonstrate that the possibility exist of technologically simulating mental illness. Medical doctors are on the front lines of fielding the complaints of "hearing voices" as they present to family practice clinics and eventually psychiatric offices. It is my opinion that the medical community is largely ignorant of these technological advancements. The adage that the patient hearing voices that their physician cannot hear is delusional until proven otherwise no longer holds true. In this book I've demonstrated the government's willingness to experiment on the general public as well as the factual existence of technology with the capability of inducing perceived auditory hallucinations. Perhaps the medical community, when confronted with patients complaining of suspected surveillance and "hearing voices," should rule out a criminal etiology as well as a psychiatric one. There are currently too many people voicing complaints of stalking, surveillance, and auditory harassment that are strikingly identical for it to be delusional disorder or psychosis in every case. While I do not deny that these disorders exist, I am merely suggesting that, with our known history on nonconsensual experimentation, we entertain causes of auditory hallucinations other than mental illness in some cases.

CHAPTER 6

Organized Stalking

"Keeping a close watch on him, they sent spies,
who pretended to be honest."

–Luke 20:20

I n January 2008 the U.S. Department of Justice (DOJ) publicized its survey: "Stalking Victimization in the United States." The results were alarming! Complaints of stalking, legitimate enough to be included in the study, were up exponentially from the previous survey done in 1996. An estimated 3.4 million people were victims of stalking while another 2.4 were victims of harassment. The study covers victimization occurring in 2005 and the first half of 2006 and inquired about events in the previous 12 months. 6% of the 5.8 million total suffered electronic monitoring such as spyware, bugging, or video surveillance. While many of the victims were stalked by someone they were acquainted with, one in ten victims were stalked and harassed by people unknown to them. The study defined stalking as a course of conduct directed at a specific person that would cause a reasonable person to feel fear. Approximately 130,000 victims reported that they were fired or asked to leave their jobs because of the stalking.

Another study, published in the American Journal of

Preventative Medicine in 2006, found that 7 million women and 2 million men in the United States have been stalked. The study was from the National Center for Injury Prevention and the Centers for Disease Control and Prevention. It also found that individuals who were never married, separated, widowed, or divorced experienced significantly higher rates of stalking then those individuals living with a partner. A 2002 study found no gender differences in the mental health effects of stalking. Both male and female victims experienced equal rates of impaired health, depression and injury, and were more likely to engage in substance abuse than their non-stalked peers.

A common theme among several of the stalking studies was the inability of the victims to get appropriate help from law enforcement officials. Despite anti-stalking laws in just about every state, victims that report stalkers are often disregarded by their local police departments as "head cases" or suffering from the delusion of being stalked. Prosecution rates bear out this fact. Between 85.4% and 93.6% of stalking perpetrators are not prosecuted and only 56.3% of those convicted are sentenced to jail. Moreover, the 2008 DOJ study reported that the most common police response to the stalking complaints was to take a report, while in 20% of the cases no action was taken at all. About 50% of victims perceived no change in the stalking or harassment after police were contacted. Obviously, we have a growing problem with stalking and harassment in the country, based upon several governmental studies. However, I would propose that the problem is compounded by the lack of appropriate law enforcement engagement at the local level. This may be due to several factors: 1) the reporting officer's perception of the victims as mentally ill for believing that they are being stalked, 2) ignorance on the part of local law enforcement as to the extent of the problem, 3) difficulty at obtaining enough evidence to justify an arrest, 4) knowledge on the part of law enforcement officials as to the difficulty in prosecuting stalking cases, 5) unwillingness to dedicate the manpower needed to investigate what they perceive as a "low-level" crime.

Armed with some basic statistics in hand, we can now turn our attention to a very specific form of stalking. Many of the victims of auditory harassment also complain of a form of stalking referred to as "organized stalking", "gang-stalking", or "cause-stalking". I prefer the term "organized stalking" as it more accurately reflects the true nature of the phenomenon. Organized stalking is the harassment of an individual by people unknown to them for the sole purpose of inducing psychological trauma. It is perpetrated by individuals from within their community working in concert with each other to achieve a desired goal and is centrally directed and organized. Gang-stalking is a term often used for this phenomenon; however, it is misleading in that it invokes a mental picture of thugs in matching jackets perpetuating the crime. This is not the case. Cause-stalking, a term coined by author David Lawson in his similarly titled book, implies a racial or social agenda on the part of the perpetrators. Again, this has not been shown to be an accurate term according to victim demographics. Surveys conducted by the human rights organization, Freedom from Covert Harassment and Surveillance, have demonstrated a relatively random distribution of victims of this crime. There appears to be no increased predilection based upon race, religion, profession, or culture. The only two common threads among the reported victims are female gender and a high incident of sexual assault facilitated with date-rape drugs such as rohypnol or GHB. A large number of male victims have also reported being raped after surreptitiously ingesting date rape drugs. Those sexual assaults go largely unprosecuted due to the amnestic effects of the various date-rape drugs as well as the narrow window of opportunity to detect them in the urine of the victim.

Organized stalking consists of a complex myriad of actions on the part of the perpetrator that has undoubtedly contributed to the rise in complaints reported by the DOJ. The problem has become so pervasive that a multitude of websites have arisen to educate and console the growing number of victims. Eleanor White has been battling the organized stalking phenomenon longer than anyone. Her website www.raven1.net is both educational and current in its content. Gangstalkingworld.com is another excellent website providing educational articles for those who suspect they may be victims of this cowardly crime.

Some of the antics associated with organized stalking include: 1) following the targeted individual 24/7 wherever they travel, 2) loitering around their homes or businesses they frequent, 3) breaking into the target's home, usually to vandalize it and rummage through their belongings with rare property theft, 4) harassing the victim with profanity or vulgar gestures while in public places, 5) character assassination of the victim through spreading rumors about them to neighbors or employers, 6) damage to a victims vehicles and /or personal property, 7) bombard the victim with loud noises around the home or work. The perpetrators will often enlist the help of victim's neighbors by convincing them that they are some form of legitimate law enforcement. In several instances the perpetrators have produced false FBI credentials to convince neighbors that they are assisting in a legitimate investigation. Often, vacant homes or apartments around the victim will be used as a base from which to terrorize the intended target. The stalking protocol used by the perpetrators is not to be confused as actual surveillance. It is simply a harassment tool used in a form of psychological warfare. The stalking is intended to induce psychological stress, alienate the victim, isolate the victim, and maintain them in a perpetual state of helplessness or victim mentality. The complaint of this type of stalking to law enforcement is often ignored or the victim is referred to a mental health professional. The psychiatric community, being ill-educated on this topic, invariably diagnoses the victim with schizophrenia or delusional disorder. The eventual discreditation of the victim, through the diagnosis of a mental disorder, is probably the ultimate intended goal of the perpetrators. This type of stalking is not a new phenomenon and gets it roots from an FBI operation called COINTELPRO.

Between 1956 and 1971 the FBI directed a number of covert operations known as COINTELPRO, an acronym for "counter intelligence program." Their goal was to infiltrate and subvert certain social and political groups that were deemed as a threat to national security. The directives governing COINTELPRO were issued by FBI director J. Edgar Hoover and were designed to "expose, disrupt, misdirect, discredit and neutralize" the activities of the targeted groups and their leaders. Some of the groups included communist organizations, women's rights groups, black nationalists, civil rights organizations, the NAACP, the American Indian Movement, and the KKK. The methods employed by the FBI are identical to those being used today by organized stalking groups. They include public character assignation, harassment through legal and financial institutions, conspicuous surveillance, illegal breaking and entering, psychological operations, vandalism, and assault. Harassment is often through the manipulation of employers, parents, neighbors, or landlords to assist in the victimization of the intended target.

COINTELPRO remained secret until 1971 when an FBI field office was broken into and documents relating to COINTELPRO

Operations were leaked to the press. In 1976 an investigation was launched by the Select Committee to Study Governmental Operations with Respect to Intelligence Activities of the United States Senate. This was chaired by Senator Frank Church and is referred to as the Church Committee Hearings. The final report of the Church Committee essentially found the FBI guilty of "vigilante operations aimed squarely at preventing the exercise of First Amendment rights of speech and association." "Unsavory and victims tactics have been employed, including anonymous attempts to break up marriages, disrupt meetings, estrange persons from their professions and provoke target groups into rivalries that might result in deaths." These tactics are identical to the ones being used by organized stalking groups today.

So the question remains, is organized stalking a continuation of COINTELPRO or merely a replication of its tactics by criminal groups? My personal belief is that it is a combination of both hypotheses. Certainly, there are several cases I am aware of where former intelligence agencies employees are being directly harassed by their former employers in a COINTELPRO fashion. However, most victims of organized stalking are not whistle-blowers or former intelligence agency employees that would awaken the ire of the intelligence community. The majority of victims are citizens with no ties to radical groups. However, the identification of one of the stalking groups in Texas leads me to the belief that this phenomenon is a combination of formal COINTELPRO training and replication of the tactics by criminals. The organization identified in San Antonio, Texas as "hiring out" this type of harassment is licensed as a private investigative agency. The agency is owned by a former FBI agent in his seventies, who would have been in his prime as an FBI agent during COINTELPRO. His employees, however, are not connected to any particular government agency and are simply licensed private investigators. Despite multiple complaints to the Texas Department of Public Safety, the licensing agency for Private Investigators, this group continues to victimize people in Texas uninhibitedly. Many former FBI agents turn to private investigative work after separating from the agency and this may be the mode of networking among the various stalking groups from state to state.

When one analyzes the complaints being voiced by victims of organized stalking from each state, striking similarities are very apparent. All of the victims are experiencing stalking, break-ins, appliance tampering and remote neural monitoring. The stalking groups are obviously networking with each other or following a template of proven successful tactics. Networking among these organized stalking groups would also explain the continuation of a victim's suffering, even after moving to another state to escape their torment. Victims who relocate, hoping to end their stalking, usually report 2-3 months of relief before the harassment resumes in their new geographic location. While the idea of multiple COINTELPRO trained agents scattered over the United States seems far-fetched at first, one need look no further than to a new alarming trend within the intelligence community for a possible answer. We will cover the role that private intelligence contractors possibly play in this phenomenon in a later chapter.

CHAPTER 7
Directed Energy

"And he performed great and miraculous signs, even causing fire to come down from heaven to earth in full view of men."
—Revelation 13:13

Complaints of attack by unseen weapons that cause burning of the skin, involuntary muscle movements, heart rate irregularities, and headache have become fairly commonplace across the United States. In many instances these complaints are in conjunction with complaints of the other modalities previously mentioned such as remote neural monitoring and stalking. Of course, psychiatrists have largely dismissed these complaints as psychosis or delusional disorder of a persecutory type; however, the number of people coming forward with these complaints and their striking similarities alluded to a more technologic etiology rather than a psychiatric one. While most psychiatrists are well versed in the diagnostic criteria for the various mental illnesses, they are largely ignorant of the recent advances in the field of directed energy. The rest of the medical community is equally ignorant of advances in this field as well as in denial regarding the continuation of nonconsensual experimentation in this country. In this chapter the reader will be introduced to the basics of directed energy as it applies to our current non-lethal weapons research programs. Although there is much overlap between the technologies used for audio harassment, remote neural monitoring, and directed energy weapons, it is best understood by individualizing them as separate entities. However the reader should realize that the same technologies used for audio harassment, for instance, may be modified for use as a weapon to cause pain rather than harassment.

For some time now research has been in progress to perfect directed energy as a form of projectile-free warfare. The terminology used in this research is similar to the terminology used in traditional ballistic research. The key elements of both are the analysis of propagation and target interaction and maximize the effectiveness of the respective weapon. Regardless of whether one is studying a projectile fired from a rifle or a laser fired from a satellite, the technology is relatively the same. Weapons are devices which deliver sufficient energy to targets to damage them. The effectiveness of the desired damage to a target is a result of the propagation and accuracy of the weapon as well as the physical properties of the target. An effective design maximizes the ease of propagation and accuracy to effect change on a known target. Directed energy fits the bill in many ways as the absolutely perfect design. The ability to fight a war without bombs or bullets is upon us. Economic constraints have limited the widespread use of directed-energy in the theater of war with favor given to traditional ballistic weapons and the large sums of money that they generate. However most traditional weapons manufacturers have initiated research and development programs into directed energy modalities; seeing them as an inevitable progression of modern warfare. We will examine the basics of directed energy as well as the possibility that some of its current experimentation is being done nonconsensually on the public. As stated before, the technology behind directed energy weaponry is closely related, if not synonymous to, the technology behind behavioral control and audio harassment.

The term "directed-energy" encompasses a variety of weapons such as lasers, particle beams and microwaves. A fourth modality of directed energy weaponry is referred to as "scalar wave" technology and is sufficiently unique from the other three to be discussed separately. Nonetheless, all directed energy weapons must deliver sufficient energy to a target to effect destruction of the target. This requires an understanding of the prospective target, whether animate or inanimate, as to the energy requirement to destroy the target. Furthermore, for a target to be affected, the energy must be effectively delivered to the target. The term for this is "propagation." Just as a bullet is subject to drag secondary to atmospheric conditions, lasers and microwaves may be subject to atmospheric moisture and other particles that inhibit their propagation. Knowing the physical characteristics of the target allows for the over-production of energy in the weapon system, so that atmospheric drag may be overcome and the appropriate amount of energy deposited at the target. Obviously, less energy would be required to degrade the performance of a target than to completely neutralize or destroy it. The amount of energy deposited is most commonly expressed in Joules. A Joule is approximately the energy required to lift a quart of milk a distance of three feet. Targets are described as either "soft" or "hard" depending on the choice of either degrading them or destroying them respectively. Determining the energy required to degrade the performance of a soft target is much more different than determining the energy required to destroy it. In order to inflict a perturbation in function, specifics about the target must be determined. For instance, in biologic systems one must know the physical and chemical composite as well as the neural anatomy and neuron depolarization frequencies. In electronic systems, the target's circuitry must be understood in order to degrade its performance rather than destroy it. Destroying a target produces immediate feedback while degrading a target requires time to observe the desired changes in the target's functioning. This may explain the long duration of time, sometimes a decade or more, that we see victims of nonconsensual directed energy experimentation enduring.

Deposition of energy alone is not sufficient to degrade or destroy a chosen target. One must also consider the factors that influence energy density as well as the energy delivery rate. The area over which the energy is delivered as well as the time in which it is delivered determines destructive effect. A small amount of energy delivered to a small area over a short period of time will be more effective than a large amount of energy delivered starting over a large area. An artillery shell is a good example of this principle. A bomb dropped one mile from a target may lose its effect through dissipation of energy while an artillery shell shot at the target from a mile away will deliver destructive energy. The same is true for directed-energy. Short pulses of energy directed at small areas may have significant effects while larger energy levels that are delivered over a large area may cause little effect. The lack of effect is a result of dissipation of the energy applied. Energy may be dissipated through condition, convection and radiation. In human systems, thermal conduction will defend against directed energy attack. As heat increases in the tissues secondary to energy deposition, cooler surrounding tissues will absorb some of the heat through conduction. After this conductivity is maximized, thermal effects will be seen at the target area. Hence, cold gel packs will increase the conductive substrate near the energy deposition area will provide some protection and require a higher energy level to be achieved by the respective weapon. Convection is similar to conduction.

Dissipation through convection access where the heat generated in a target is lost to cooler ambient temperatures around the target. Indeed, this is also seen in human systems. The effect of a given energy level is lessened in an ambient environment that includes cold moving air around the target. Radiation of energy occurs after the target's ability to lessen the effect through conduction and convection is overcome. Depending on the applied energy level, this may inhibit destruction but will not inhibit degradation. An example of this is a vehicle sitting in a sunny parking lot. A peak interior temperature will eventually be met where the energy radiating away from the vehicle is equal to the energy applied. The temperature increases within the vehicle will cease without destroying the vehicle; however, the interior components will show signs of degradation. Obviously, these principles deal with the thermal effects produced by directed-energy which coincide with the subjective feeling of discomfort or pain in human systems. However, there may be non-thermal effects upon biologic systems produced by directed energy as well that do not necessarily obey these principles.

Directed energy induces thermal effects in biologic and non-biologic systems through its ability to increase the heat content in the targeted system. The amount of energy deposited, the target characteristics, and its ability to dissipate the heat generated are directly related to the eventual outcome of destruction or degradation. However, in biologic systems there are also non-thermal effects that may incapacitate the target regardless of the thermal effects. These are biologic effects that energy and non-ionizing radiation have on the various systems of the body. Much of this data has come from cell phone exposure studies and microwave energy research. Weapons such as the Active Denial System operate at 94 GHz and other high powered microwave systems operate between 1-3 GHz, cell phones emit microwave radiation at similar frequencies. Some groups have reported blood brain barrier defects and nerve cell death with exposure in these ranges. Chronic exposure to low levels of radio-frequency in the microwave range, have been found to cause cancer in several animal models despite thermal effects. However, the studies are inconclusive as to how this relates to human subjects. Majorities of cell phone exposure studies in the United States are sponsored by cell phone companies and are subject to bias. European Studies tend to report the hazards while American studies suppress them. Other non-thermal effects that have been reported include changes in the immune system, neurologic effects, behavioral effects, potentiation of drug effects across the blood-brain barrier, and calcium efflux in the brain tissue. All of these findings have been reported by both European and American researchers, with calcium ion efflux being the most reproducible. The biological significance of this finding remains to be seen.

Two other hallmark features related to electromagnetic field exposure are tinnitus and the sensation of magnetophosphenes. These are mentioned separately due to their prevalence among those suspected of having nonconsensual exposure. Tinnitus is the presence of sound within the inner ear without a corresponding external source. It is most commonly caused by exposure to loud sounds and aging. The prevalence rate for tinnitus in the United States is 1 in 22 people or approximately 4.50% within the general population. Among those people who report a subjective sense of electromagnetic sensitivity, the rate is much higher. In one study, 89 electromagnetically hypersensitive patients were compared to 107 non-hypersensitive controls. The finding of tinnitus was 50.72 % among the hypersensitive group as opposed to 17.5 % in the control group. This study suggests a link between EMF exposure and tinnitus. Moreover, nearly 90% of individuals who report suspected nonconsensual experimentation with electromagnetic weapons report tinnitus. In either case, this may be induced by the creation of a small electric current within the auditory cortex by varying magnetic fields. A similar effect is seen in the eyes. Magnetophosphenes are streaks of light that can be seen with the eyelids closed during exposure to magnetic fields. It is well understood that electronic currents applied directly to the body can stimulate muscle and nerve tissue. However, it has also been shown that exposure to extremely low frequency electric and magnetic fields can induce currents within the body at levels lower than those that can stimulate peripheral nerve tissue. It has been found that the integrative properties of the synapses and neural networks of the central nervous system render cognitive function sensitive to the effects of weak electric fields, below the threshold for peripheral nerve stimulation. Magnetophosphenes are an example of this. Weak electromagnetic fields are postulated to affect voltage-gated ion channels that cause electric current to discharge within the optic system. This sensitivity to weak magnetic fields makes the central nervous system particularly vulnerable to even weak pulses of directed energy. Nearly 100% of those who allege nonconsensual exposure to directed energy report sleep deprivation secondary to magnetophosphenes.

For any target, animate or inanimate, to be interacted with, the energy must first reach the target. Propagation is what determines how efficiently energy reaches the intended target. Propagation is dependent on energy loss and energy spread. Energy spread occurs whether both the weapon and the target are on earth or in the vacuum of space. Energy loss occurs as the energy interacting with a physical medium, such as interaction with the atmosphere when either the weapon or the targets are in the atmosphere. Even directed energy weapons have a small amount of energy spread inherent to their design. For example, a laser will have some amount of beam divergence due to refraction of light. Beam divergence can be partially accommodated for with adaptive optics. All forms of directed energy may have energy spread through heating the surrounding atmosphere causing divergence within this beam channel and nonlinear effects. This is minimized by creating a beam channel between two parallel laser beams which create plasma through which the desired beam may pass more readily unobstructed. This is not true in the vacuum of space. Electromagnetic waves do not need a physical medium to propagate and will travel at the speed of light in a vacuum. Obviously, propagation through the atmosphere has many more variables associated with it such as aerosol content, water vapor content, and amount of particulate matter. However, extensive research has been done to overcome these variables for each type of directed energy weapon.

Lasers have been the most troublesome of the directed energies to weaponize due to energy loss and spread problems. However, it has been done. High energy laser systems have been produced for missile defense systems mounted on ships, planes, and ground installations. In 2010, the Los Angeles County Prison System announced that they would be putting into use a laser system to control unruly prisoners. The ceiling mounted device would allow deputies to target difficult prisoners with a joystick controller to inflict a painful burn in order to control them. In reality, laser is only used in this system for target acquisition and is not the modality causing the burning sensation. The system, called the Assault Intervention Device, is similar to other systems called the Active Denial System and Silent Guardian Protection System. All are manufactured by Raytheon and all use millimeter wave technology to inflict a painful stimulus that causes the target to move out of the path of the beam. Millimeter

waves move at the speed of light and penetrate skin to a depth
of 1/64 of an inch causing thermal pain in dermal nerve endings.
The range, depending on the system used, may be between
250 meters and 500 meters. Microwave and millimeter wave
technology as it relates to the weaponry has been extensively
researched. Much of what appears to be either criminal use of
this technology or nonconsensual experimentation with it seems
to be comprised of millimeter wave or microwave modalities.

Microwaves and millimeter waves cause damage by inducing
heat. Oxygen and water will both absorb microwave energy and
radiate heat while leaving a ceramic container cool to the touch.
Everyone has noted this fact while heating water for coffee or tea
in a microwave oven. Microwave photon energies are small and
as a result will pass through most insulating materials. However,
their frequency is quite low, less than 100 GHz, therefore most
metals reflect them. Indeed, the DoD protects their electronic
equipment by encasing them in metal boxes. For example, the
control centers for the unmanned predator drones are encased
in metallic cargo containers for protection from this type of
directed energy attack. In theory, a suit of aluminum foil would
shield from millimeter or microwave weapon attack. However,
folding and cornering of most thin malleable metal shielding
results in micro-tears where the target would still be vulnerable
to attack. One DOD official stated that, "if you're going to
make a metal suit to protect from microwaves, you'd be better
off making it out of steel so you would be bulletproof as well."
An interesting observation of microwaves is that they will skip
across ocean surfaces extending their range well beyond that
intended when beamed at the earth from space. While salt water
is a good conductor of electrical current, it reflects microwaves
in a manner similar to metallic surfaces. Furthermore, due to
their large wavelength, microwave propagation does not rely on

adaptive optics for beam correction as lasers do for long range applications. This is fortunate, since otherwise microwaves would not have found so many applications in communications where accurate phase and amplitude information is required for a coherent signal to be received.

Before their use against biologic targets, microwaves were developed for use against electronic targets. Electronic equipment is particularly vulnerable to microwave attack. The thin strips of wire, semiconductors and circuitry etched onto a circuit board, can be easily heated to the point of destruction. Circuit boards are designed with the some over-heating in mind. Heat sinks are incorporated into the board material that allow for normal dissipation of heat when normal currents are applied. On a printed circuit board, the wiring may be less than a micrometer in thickness and width. A current of less than a milliamp may be sufficient to melt conducting paths on a circuit board. As electronic technology tends toward smaller and more compact circuits, designs have less space available to incorporate heat sinks or voltage escape pathways. Thus our trend toward miniaturization of electronic components is making them significantly more vulnerable to directed energy attack.

Electronic equipment is attacked in two ways, through in-band and out-of-band attacks. In-band damage is accomplished through directing a frequency of energy at the chosen target within its normal operating band. This type of attack enters through antennas or openings in the targeted device. The device itself may amplify the incoming signal causing further destruction. For this reason, military radar equipment is designed to frequency hop so intentionally harmful frequencies directed at the equipment cannot be maliciously received. An out-of-band attack involves an attack on a target with energy not within its operating frequency. The damage is affected by applying raw power to the target in order to override its circuitry. A good example of this is a lightning strike in which non-surge protected devices in the home are destroyed when the home is hit with lightning. To protect from this type of damage, the military houses sensitive equipment in microwave reflective metallic containers. However, microwaves will still enter through windows or gaps in the protective surface. Moreover, when microwaves enter through small apertures they are strongly diffracted and can irradiate an area thought to be adequately protected. Depending on the magnitude of the offending frequency, targets may be destroyed, rendered dysfunctional, or controlled.

Particle beams are composed of atomic and subatomic particles and propagate at near the speed of light. Their interactions with each other and a target must be understood on a basis of atomic physics, nuclear physics, and relativity. There are two types of known particle beams: charged and neutral. A charged particle beam is made up of particles such as electrons or protons while a neutral particle beam is composed of atomic hydrogen and neutrinos. The electrical field of particle beams interacts with existing magnetic fields and vice-versa. This interaction, described by Maxwell's Equations of Electromagnetic Theory, is responsible for the propagation of electric and magnetic fields coupled together as electromagnetic radiation. Charged particles tend to have a repulsive effect on each other and thus cause beam divergence while the electrical current they produce cause a beam contraction. The repulsive force dominates the electrical attractive force which makes neutral particle beams more useful in a vacuum. Atmospheric conditions minimize the repulsive forces of a charged particle beam. As a particle beam propagates through the atmosphere, collisions with molecules of oxygen, nitrogen and water vapor occur. A neutral beam becomes ionized, losing electrons that make it neutral and increasing divergence. However, a charged beam that propagates through the atmosphere undergoes charge neutralization which eliminates beam expansion through electrostatic repulsion. As the ionized particles in a charged beam enter the atmosphere, the surrounding air becomes ionized, going from a neutral gas to ionized plasma. The charged electrons and nuclei in the atmospheric plasma are free to carry electrical current. Therefore, the utility of particle beams as weapons fall into two categories: neutral beams for use in space and charged beams for use within the atmosphere. Particle beams release x-rays upon interaction with a target which is part of their inherent danger.

The latest form of directed energy to be extensively researched is scalar energy. To date, many physicists doubt the existence of scalar waves; however, every industrialized nation is actively researching them. Scalar waves do not obey Maxwell's Equations which govern most electromagnetic waves and are thus hard to describe as a propagating wave form. Some researchers describe them as static points of light which are activated by a transfer of energy while others describe them as traveling faster than the speed of light. Field theory dictates that energy decreases from the point of transmission of most types of waves up to its point of reception by a receiver; thus, received power is generally lower than the originally transmitted power. This is not true for scalar waves. There is no attenuation of power during transmission of scalar waves. Therefore, scalar waves provide for the wireless transfer of electrical energy. Many physicists have suggested that this would only be possible in the vacuum of space. However, researcher Konstantin Meyl has demonstrated the effects of a scalar wave in the atmosphere. His research has shown that scalar waves propagate at 1.5 times the speed of light, transfer energy to a receiver, and are not attenuated by an anechoic chamber.

Scalar wave technology has a profound impact on possible nonconsensual experimentation with this type of directed energy. Many of the people voicing complaints of directed energy exposure have tried shielding themselves with anechoic chambers to no avail. Furthermore, investigators have reported using spectrum analyzers to scan alleged victims homes for extraneous radio frequencies, only to find untraceable wave forms and energy level increases. These findings suggest that some of the current experimentation may be scalar based or at least may be using scalar waves to modulate other wave forms through most forms of known shielding materials. In a correspondence with Konstantin Meyl, it was suggested that victims finding no relief from anechoic chambers should be suspicious of the possible use of scalar technology.

In conclusion, the preceding chapter on directing energy is solely meant to touch the surface of this technology for the naïve reader. Those readers with physics background or further interest in the topic can certainly find information on directed energy that is written in more technical terms. For the purpose of this book, I wanted to introduce the reader to technology that may be unfamiliar to them. It is important that the public become aware of this technology due to its increased use on the private sector. During the writing of this book several alarming deployments of directed energy technology on the public occurred. Several cities saw the use of long range acoustic devices (LRADS) by local law enforcement agencies to institute crowd control. The LRAD emits a disorienting beam of sound at targets causing them to clear out of a desired perimeter. It was used at the G20 Summit in Pittsburg and British Columbia as well as on a crowd in San Diego, California. A millimeter wave weapon produced by Raytheon is currently being tested in a Los Angeles prison. Millimeter waves, which cause a burning sensation in the skin, are being remotely controlled by prison guards to alter the behavior of uncooperative prisoners. Identical to the Army's Active Denial System, the burning sensation caused by millimeter waves induces the target to move out of the direction of the beam. The burning sensation ceases once the target moves out of the beam's direction. If this technology seems futuristic to you, then the future has arrived with the potential to worsen exponentially.

CHAPTER 8

Targeted Individuals

"They were allowed to torment them for five months,
but not kill them, and their torment was like the torment
of a scorpion when it stings someone."

–Revelation 9:5

A ssuming the government's intelligence agencies and DoD haven't suddenly started obeying the legal guidelines of the Common Rule or the moral suggestions of the Nuremberg Code, one subset of the population does seem to be suffering as unwitting guinea pigs of government sponsored experimentation. Given the United States Government's history of using the public in nonconsensual experimentation, it would be illogical to think that they have suddenly stopped, especially when much of the technology being currently tested can be used remotely. For decades, beginning with MKULTRA and its related projects, the governments of most of the industrialized nations have been searching for reliable ways to control the masses. While most of us are familiar with the control that can be gained through guns, taxes and the media, few are familiar with the weapons mentioned in this book that rely on the electromagnetic spectrum. Fewer still understand the strange susceptibility that the human nervous system has to electromagnetic energy. Throughout history certain segments of the population have felt the need to separate themselves from government and thrive based upon their own self-reliance. The Amish religious sect is an excellent example of this, although they have succumbed somewhat to governmental intrusion through allowing their children to attend the public school system. This single allowance has reduced the number of individuals remaining in the sect, however, secondary to exposure of their youth to modernization. Other fringe religious groups, as well as survivalist organizations, have also fled to rural areas to escape the ever watching eye of Big Brother. Until recently, escaping to agricultural areas, where one could live off the land, one could successfully remove themselves from "the grid". However, the relative resistance of these groups to the traditional control mechanisms of taxation, bureaucracy, and the media did eventually invoke the ire of the federal government. Labeled as potential domestic terrorists, many of these groups have been infiltrated by FBI agents for closer observation. In several extreme cases of governmental intervention, these groups were forced to comply with governmental control by force. The reader may remember the tragedies that occurred at Ruby Ridge and the Branch Davidian compound where government agencies did resort to force to disrupt these groups. The federal government, realizing that the American public would not continue to tolerate armed attacks on its citizens, began to look for more covert ways to exercise control over these agriculturally independent populations. This is not to infer that the individuals suffering at the hands of current technological experimentation fit in the category of separatists. In most cases they do not appear to be separatists, radicals or anti-government. I am merely attempting to explain, from a governmental viewpoint, their plausible need to develop more sophisticated means of controlling the population. The governments from every industrialized nation no longer seek to merely govern their people. The emphasis has changed from governing populations to controlling populations with the United Nations helping pave the way through a myriad of programs.

The group, feeling the brunt of this slow conversion from representative to mental totalitarianism refers to themselves as target individuals or "T.I.s." This rapidly growing group of individuals is the one voicing the complaints of exposure to electromagnetic technologies meant to alter cognition and physiology. While many of these accounts could've been written off as mental illness a decade ago the frequency and similarity of the complaints being vocalized currently point toward a much different etiology. The lack of legislation against nonconsensual experimentation, the willingness of the government to participate in nonconsensual experimentation and the known research and development of electromagnetic weapons validate these claims as probable covert experimentation. I have interviewed thousands of the people voicing these complaints both alone and through Freedom from Covert Surveillance and Harassment, an advocacy organization offering support to the victims. My descriptions of the experiences of these "targeted individuals" are based upon my interviews as well as statistical data provided by FFCHS through extensive surveys that they regularly conduct. Of note, FFCHS is not the only support group that has formed. Many other support groups have developed to handle the exponentially growing number of complaints that are being voiced.

After several thousand interviews and many hours of mulling over questionnaires filled out by victims, I have pieced together an explanation of their experiences. The reader has probably noticed that I do not refer to the victims with descriptive terms like "alleged" or "probable." After completing this book the reader will be equally convinced that this is a real phenomenon that is destroying the lives of thousands of individuals and their families. Undoubtedly, many victims and non-victims alike will disagree with some of my findings and descriptions of this phenomenon. However, while some victims may have circumstances that differ slightly from my template, the overwhelming majority are experiencing a very methodical progression of experimentation that fits well into the template that I am hypothesizing. Targeted individuals are experiencing a form of experimentation that follows a progression of phases that include selection, surveillance, stalking, defamation, attack, and monitoring. These six phases may have some overlap; however, they are distinct enough to separate them into phases. The time spent on each phase may vary from individual to individual and is probably a reflection of the desires of the perpetrator of the experimentation. Again, the description is based upon a compilation of data and counter-intelligence gathered from surveillance of a perpetrator group identified in San Antonio, Texas. The group in Texas that was counter-surveilled has been independently identified by four unrelated victims from four different geographic areas of Texas.

Selection of a target may be for a myriad of reasons at the local level. One must remember this technology is not available to the average person. The groups perpetrating this type of experimentation are given access to the technology as covert, independent contractors of the government agencies responsible for its development. This research is a continuation of earlier behavioral control operations which were mostly done through front companies. The current experimentation is no different. The groups given access to the technology are allowed to choose victims for any reason they deem necessary. The agencies behind the technology are merely interested in collecting the data on its successes or failures. Therefore, as the data is collected at the top from each of the many perpetrator groups, the selection of victims probably appears random. The selection demographics look very different at the local level.

While a small number of victims have come forward with convincing evidence of direct harassment from various government agencies, these are mostly whistle-blowers employed by the same agencies and comprised the minority. Most victims are everyday people who would be considered "common" by most standards. Through interviews and questionnaires, we have found some trends among the victim population. A large percentage of the victims are female. Most of these female victims have reported drug facilitated rape and sexual assault. This is probably not a part of the experimentation as much as a representation of the criminal nature of the perpetrator group. Technology that allows for complete surveillance, stalking, and subliminal control makes sexual assault a very easy crime to accomplish. While rape has been used in the past as a part of mental programming through trauma, it appears that it is seen more as a "perk" among the current experimental perpetrators. Nonetheless, it is no less physically traumatic and psychologically damaging to the victim. One group of victims in Palm Springs, California does appear to be targeted sexually. This group of mostly gay men is being audibly harassed by the same female voice through the microwave auditory effect as well as being victimized through drug assisted sexual assault. Obviously this represents a psychological hatred on the part of the group perpetuating these crimes in that area. However, to summarize, the selection of targets for inclusion into this experimental protocol may be specific at the local level with some aspect of particular traits that are sought out by the perpetrators. At the agency level, where the data is ultimately compiled, each perpetrator group's inclusion criteria probably average out to give the target population a random appearance.

Surveillance of the chosen target closely follows selection. The surveillance phase differs from the stalking phase in that during the surveillance phase the target is unaware that it is occurring. Once selected, the target is extensively surveilled through multiple means which include background checks, credit checks, mail tampering, email hacking and direct observation, both physically and electronically. Surveillance accomplishes several important goals that are integral to the success of the remainder of the operation. It allows the perpetrator to accurately determine the target's daily living activities. Most importantly, where they live, work, bank and how they spend their leisure time are quickly assessed. The people they spend the majority of their time with are identified and scaled in order of importance. For instance, highly valued circumferential targets would include the target's close family members, supervisors, physicians, clergy and anyone else that they may spend substantial time communicating with. This allows the perpetrators to know with reasonable certainty who the target will confide in once they are aware of their targeting. During this phase the target's social status is ascertained with regard to their relationships with loved ones, neighbors, co-workers, supervisors, and others. Any participation in taboo behavior such as drug use, excessive alcohol intake, domestic violence, infidelity or pornography are especially noted and followed up on very closely. All the data collected during this phase will be used to control, mislead, defame, and isolate the target. Also, during this phase the perpetrators will often have neighbors, co-workers and relatives assisting them with the surveillance. This is usually accomplished by misleading those individuals into thinking they are assisting with a legitimate law enforcement investigation. In one instance the private investigative agency perpetuating the surveillance identified themselves to a target's neighbor as FBI agents, complete with fraudulent identification badges. One would be very surprised at the number of people who fall for this ploy without even asking for appropriate identification or contacting the alleged agency to inquire if the surveillance is legitimate. Ignorance of the laws, both nationally and at the state level, regarding surveillance and right to privacy, make this a very effective ploy. The successful application of this technique by the perpetrators will later legitimize the defamation phase and protect them from possible arrest during the stalking phase. With the neighbors believing that they are assisting with an investigation by a legitimate agency, they are more apt to believe the defamatory remarks they are told about the target. Moreover, they are less likely to call the police and report the vehicles they see parked in front of the target's home throughout the night.

Stalking of the target is a natural extension of the surveillance phase. These phases differ in that the surveillance phase is usually unknown to the target while the stalking phase is done with full awareness of the target. In current literature, the stalking phase of this type of victimization is usually described as gang stalking, organized stalking, or cause-stalking. Gang stalking and cause-stalking are inaccurate descriptions in that they imply either street gang involvement or some grandiose reasoning behind the stalking. Organized stalking is probably the most accurate description, reflecting the highly organized and methodically planned out form of stalking that these victims experience. The methods involved are directly adapted from the COINTELPRO operations ran by the FBI in the 1950's and 1960's against groups seen as radical elements. The tactics include total inundation of the target at home and wherever they may go, breaking and entering of their domicile and physical harassment and intimidation. Electronic harassment is used during this phase with regard to email tampering, computer hacking, cell phone spoofing and cyber-bullying. More exotic forms of electronic harassment are covered as part of the attack phase but may be present in any phase of this type of victimization.

The stalking phase serves several important functions for the group perpetuating the operation to insure that the target is totally enveloped in the operation with minimal chance of escape. It places the victim in a victim-mind state of hopelessness, especially once the victim has been ignored by police agencies through which the victim has sought help. Stalking is very difficult for police agencies to prosecute under normal circumstances. Police assistance in cases of organized stalking where the victim's everyday actions have been studied through surveillance for months or years is nearly futile. In addition, the stalkers are highly trained, often with federal or local law enforcement backgrounds themselves, in pushing the envelope just short of giving the police a reason to investigate. The hopelessness that ensues from the feeling that all backs have been turned from believing or assisting the victim is integral to the success of the operation. After repeated police complaints of break-ins where nothing is stolen and personal belongings have been rifled through, the victim is labeled mentally unsound and further police complaints are ignored. Only felony burglary will be investigated by law enforcement agencies. Criminal trespassing will only result in a report that is filed away without an investigation. At worst, multiple complaints of stalking and criminal trespassing will result in a psychiatric referral or mandatory twenty-four hour psychiatric evaluation. The inability of the victim to get appropriate law enforcement assistance helps instill the belief that law enforcement is complicit in their victimization and limits them from further complaints. Once this level of hopelessness is achieved, the perpetrators feel confident in escalating their stalking to more frequent breaking and entering as well as physical and sexual assault with less risk of arrest. The victim mind state often causes the target to go into an extreme state of reclusion which furthers their chance of a psychiatric diagnosis once a psychiatric exam is requested or mandated. This part of the operation has been brilliantly designed with assistance from psychiatric professionals and is a scenario that continues to play out to perfection in almost every case.

The stalking phase serves another purpose. The victim must be located through GPS in order for the constellation of other modalities to be used on them. This can be accomplished in several different ways. Stalking may be a way of performing constant 24/7 GPS location through GPS enabled devices in the hands of the stalkers. This obviates the need for tracking chips in the victim and explains why the stalking phase almost always comes to an abrupt end with only the electronic harassment remaining. At one time chipping the target, much like GPS chipping of animals to study migratory patterns, was probably the more common scenario. However, this exposes the perpetrator group to the possibility of arrest for physical assault if caught and provides evidence of assault to the victim if the chip is found. A less risky alternative to stalking the victim close enough to remotely GPS them until their EEG can be catalogued and used through remote neural monitoring for the remainder of the operation. Our research has reinforced this fact. We have frequency scanned thousands of victims for covertly placed micro-chips with very few found on x-ray or MRI. To add to the confusion, part of the operation is apparently to convince the target that they have been chipped. This causes them to exhaust their finances looking for an embedded device that doesn't exist with such fervor that it contributes to their psychiatric diagnosis. Essentially, while chipping was once integral to the operation, it is now part of the psychological victimization. However, because many people have been complaining of this targeting for a decade or more, scanning for a tracking chip should probably be part of their work-up. Most recently, Bob Boyce, an inventor from Georgia, was allegedly chipped by an agent involved with the NSA. His chip was found on x-ray and removed by a surgeon. It was a Verichip brand chip that was covertly placed in the tissue of his lateral shoulder where it underwent malignant changes. This case is still in litigation. For the record, in an email correspondence with the makers of Verichip, they assured me that they do not condone covert chipping with their product nor will it function as a GPS tracking chip. The serial number on Boyce's chip allegedly was traced back to a lot of chips sold to the United States government. I will allow the reader to make their own decision regarding the sincerity and the reply I received from Verichip. Nonetheless, the fact that we are not routinely finding chips in the multitude of victims and the targeting continues in those with chips removed tells me that it's being done through other means with chipping or stalking being used strictly as a method of location. Dr. Robert Duncan, in Soul Catcher: Secrets of Cybernetic Warfare Revealed puts forth this same assumption.

The stalking phase takes place hand-in-hand with the defamation phase. Inevitably, the stalkers are occasionally caught and questioned by neighbors, onlookers, or possibly local law enforcement officials. The excuse most often given to those who question the stalking is that the target is under official investigation for a drug, sex, or criminal crime. Since most of this type of stalking is usually done by private investigative groups, they often have former officers on their payroll or close enough relationships with local municipalities that the police question them no further. Neighbors that have noticed the 24/7 stalking are usually receptive of the drug or sex crime excuse for the simple reason that only a legitimate agency would spend the money necessary to surveil someone "really dangerous" for twenty four hours per day. The PI groups in San Antonio, Texas would present themselves as FBI agents since their company's owner is former FBI. Neighbors or others who notice the organized stalking will almost always believe this excuse. The defamation eventually leads the target to extreme measures to deny the allegations made against them which in turn make them look that much guiltier. The defamation is much worse for licensed professionals such as doctors, lawyers, teachers, nurses or any state licensed professional. The "drug addiction" scenario is most often used in these cases where the mere mention of a drug problem will usually mandate that they undergo drug screening. Illicit drugs are usually placed in the victim's food or drinks that they are known to consume frequently through months of surveillance. Once their appropriate licensing agency is notified of their possible drug problem, the stalkers ensure that they will test positively for the drug that they are accused of abusing. This scenario works with near 100% effectiveness in destroying the career of the victim. The ultimate goal of the stalking and defamation phase is to get the target diagnosed as mentally ill or drug addicted to ensure job loss where they will be more apt to remain home where the rest of the operation can be accomplished. Incidentally, the stalking and defamation phases are also the two easiest points in this operation to intervene successfully and bring it to a halt. Unfortunately, most victims, out of fear or suspicion that they are being targeted by a legitimate investigative agency, do not pursue this. Moreover, until recently most states have had very weak anti-stalking laws that are not easily enforced. Texas has taken the lead in 2011 with a bill written by state legislator Jane Nelson and Judith Zaffirini that was passed into law. The bill was written after a young woman who complained of stalking to the Bexar County Sheriff's Department was written off as mentally ill. Her stalker had held her at gunpoint while forcing her to slit her own wrists and write a suicide letter. She survived but was largely ignored by the appropriate agencies she entrusted to help her. Several months later her stalker followed her to work and murdered her in the parking lot. According to the new law, a restraining order can be issued now against an alleged stalker without first proving bodily injury by that person or persons. Furthermore, the definition of stalking has been changed to make the charge much easier to put forth. Unfortunately, this charge did not come in time for Kristi Appleby for whom the law was changed. An organized effort should be undertaken to force every state to follow suit in altering their stalking rules. This will make defending against organized stalking much easier. Currently, the perpetrators of this type of stalking take full advantage of the lack of legislation against it.

While it appears that I am solely placing blame on independent private investigative agencies for the stalking, I am not excluding participation by corrupt individuals that are active duty law enforcement at federal and local levels. This does occur, as I will illustrate. One must remember that the technology being used to commit these crimes originates at the federal government level. Hence, it is seen being used most often by private investigative agencies that are owned and operated by former FBI agents. These individuals maintain contacts with the agency who work with them in a reciprocal relationship. These relationships are imperative to the defamation phase. The majority of the public, dumbed down by years in the American public school system, will believe the defamatory lies told about a target by the private investigators. However, the more educated members of society, who see private investigators as nothing more than licensed criminals, will question the legitimacy of what they are being told about a family member, friend, or co-worker. An active duty police officer or FBI agent spreading this same misinformation is seen as much more credible by the people being subjected to it. My own experience with defamation serves as a good example of active duty FBI employees taking part in this phase. A close friend of mine received a call on her cell phone from someone claiming to be an FBI agent, asking her to come in for questioning. The term, "asking", I am using loosely. She was actually told that she would be formally requested to come in and if she did not come in voluntarily. Fearful from the threat, she reported as instructed to the FBI office in San Antonio, Texas. After going through their metal detectors and having a copy of her driver's license made, she was greeted by an FBI agent. Special Agent J.A. questioned her extensively about my first book. A New Breed: Satellite Terrorism in America. Of course, he downplayed the existence of the technology mentioned in the book. In finishing the interview, he told her not to believe anything I talk about, that I was a "piece of shit" and she would do well to stop communicating with me. He added that I was not under any type of official investigation, inadvertently admitting that this was strictly harassment. This occurrence is my first experience with active duty FBI personnel taking part in the defamation phase. I assume that this is probably going on in other cases as well. As of the writing of this book I have yet to be questioned by this agent directly. One would surmise that questioning the author of the book would serve them better than harassing the author's friends who have only read the book. Again, the fact that they have not directly questioned me leads me to believe that their goal was purely harassment, defamation and an attempt to prevent this book from being released.

The best defense against defamation is to know your neighbors well and live a good life. Despite the stalking and attacks, one should do their best to function normally. Continue to work, attend church, children's activities or whatever social activities you would ordinarily be expected to attend. Reclusive behavior will lead people to believe the lies being told about you. Moreover, stick to victim's forums or organizations that handle victims of this type of crime to vent frustrations or talk about your experiences. Repeated attempts to convince non-believers of what you are going through will further align their belief with the doubts about your sanity that they're being told. Moreover, if you are using illicit drugs, STOP! Illicit drug use can and will be used against you, not only to defame you but the entire crime will be blamed on drug induced psychosis. The government has specifically targeted drug abusers for mind control experimentation ever since the early MKULTRA subprojects, solely for the reason that they are easily discredited. In conclusion, visibility in your community and normal societal interactions are key in defeating the defamation phase. This is a lesson learned from the perpetrators themselves. The perpetrator groups in the San Antonio area have ingrained themselves so well in their community as good Methodist, wholesome people, that I wager no one that knows them would suspect or believe the atrocities they have committed. Victims must do the same. Living your life as a recluse, placing foil in the windows and constantly talking about this issue to people who are uniformed will worsen your plight.

The attack phase is characterized by directed-energy attacks meant to disrupt normal physiologic functioning. It may occur at any time during a victim's targeting but is most noticeable as a distinct phase late in the targeting. Early attacks, prior to the victim's awareness of stalking or defamation, may be perceived as ordinary physiological medical issues. Often the victim has multiple physician visits with complaints of muscle twitching, headaches, heart palpitations, skin burning and other more obscure complaints with nothing medically abnormal found. Later in their targeting the attacks are accompanied with voice to skull transmissions that make it very obvious to the victim that their ailments are not the result of medical pathology. Once the perpetrators are certain the victim is hearing their transmissions and have noticed the stalking, the attacks will escalate. During the attack phase, the victim can expect to be assailed almost twenty-four hours per day. If the victim is lucky enough to still be employed by the time this phase begins, attacks will be used as their key weapons to sleep deprive the victim. Often, the attacks will subside just long enough for the victim to fall asleep with hopes that they will sleep through their alarm and be tardy or absent to work. Remember, the goal of this phase is complete annihilation of the victim's personal and professional life. This phase will continue until these goals are met or the perpetrator group is diverted or hired to target someone else. Manpower constraints within the perpetrator group will often result in abrupt cessation of attack as they focus their attention on another target that they've been directed or paid to attack. However, the victim will still usually have the infrequent attacks as a reminder that they are still being watched and are not entirely free from the program.

According to Dr. Robert Duncan PhD, in his book "Soul Catcher: secrets of cybernetic warfare revealed, the attacks are the result of central nervous system manipulation. In effect, the brain is being manipulated to manifest the physical symptoms of twitching, burning, spasms and other symptoms." While this may be true, almost all of the victims also report electrical disturbances within their homes. It is my belief that some of the attacks are secondary to directed energy attacks at specifically targeted peripheral nerves, muscles and organs and not strictly through the central nervous centers controlling them. In effect, the same directed energy modalities being used to open and close garage doors, turn lights on and off and disrupt computer screens in the victim's home may also be used to physically attack the victim at targeted sites other than the brain. This may explain why neuro programming to alter the EEG in most victims does stop some, but not all, of the attacks. It would stand to reason that with the myriad of weapons within the electromagnetic spectrum at their disposal, the mode of attack would be variable in nature and not dependent solely upon central nervous system manipulation.

The weapons used in the attack phase include microwave, millimeter wave, radio-frequency, laser and probably scalar modalities. All of these modalities have been researched extensively and weaponized for military use as mentioned earlier in the book. While they have all been identified under the heading of "non-lethal" weapons, non-lethality in the research setting was not based on 24/7 exposure. Moreover, the exact effect of their exposure long term on the human body is not known, at least not in official research. The victims of the current experimentation may be the guinea pigs of some type of long term exposure protocol that is too unethical to be done under a legitimate Institutional Review Board with consenting volunteers.

The attack phase is followed by the monitoring phase. Having worked with multiple victims that have been victimized for varying lengths of time, it is clear that the victims have been chosen for experimentation for the duration of their lifetime. Dr. Duncan and I are in agreement that the targeting is done for the life of the individual. However, once the goals of the perpetrators have been met, namely, social, personal and occupational destruction, the attack phase often lessens. As mentioned earlier, this victim will experience the occasional attack as a reminder to them that they are still being watched. Apparently, one of the rules of this experimental protocol is that once a victim is chosen, he or she must be monitored until their natural death occurs. Many victims are drawn to suicide by their respective perpetrators. This may be an attempt by the perpetrator groups to prematurely end the monitoring phase of one particular victim so manpower can be focused on other victims. The psychological resilience of the victim to the stress of the experimentation obviously plays a factor as well. From a medical perspective, the monitoring phase is probably to denote any immune problems, cancers, psychiatric problems or diseases that may result from the long term exposure to the electromagnetic weapons used in the experimentation. These issues will need to be elucidated before those modalities are released on the population as a whole for psycho-social control. In 1971 Dr. Jose Delgado, and MKULTRA researcher, published "Physical Control of the Mind: Toward a Psychocivilized Society." His research required implanting the brain with a micro-chip to acquire the desired results. The development of directed energy has allowed for more efficient delivery with even better results without the need for brain implantation.

CHAPTER 9

Mind Doctors

"A joyful heart is good medicine,
but a crushed spirit dries up the bones".

—Proverbs 17:22

The word "psyche" comes from ancient Greek and is interpreted as soul or butterfly. The Royal College of Psychiatrists uses the butterfly as its Coat of Arms. The term psychiatrist was first coined by physician Johann Christian Reil in 1808 to describe a medical doctor that treats the "soul." Prior to the use of the term "psychiatrist" mental illness was recognized as a disorder but treatment was often arcane and barbaric. Lunatic asylums are known to have existed as far back as 800AD in the Middle East. However, England is recognized as having built the first specialty hospital dedicated to lunacy in the 13th century. The Bethlem Royal Hospital in London was acquired by the City of London by 1547 and was operational until 1948. During most of that time the institutions were used primarily as holding cells with little to no treatment provided. It wasn't until King George III in England, who suffered from bouts of psychosis secondary to porphyria, was treated and his disease placed in remission, that mental illness was seen as treatable. A French physician, Dr. Philippe Pinel, was the first to theorize that therapeutic treatment may work in the mentally ill and is regarded as the father of modern psychiatry.

As asylums proliferated in Europe and the United States, the number of people being forced into them grew exponentially. By the early 1900's the number of people in asylums in Europe numbered in the hundreds of thousands and was approximately 150,000 in the United States in 1904. Despite the new humane treatment ideas that started the proliferations of asylums, they had once again become custodial institutions in Europe and the United States, housing both the mentally ill and the destitute.

By the early 20th century psychiatry had hit an all-time low with respect to other medical specialties. In an attempt to bolster the view of psychiatry as a legitimate medical science, two men began to attempt to classify mental illness as symptoms of other biological processes. Emil Krepelin and Karl Kahlbaum both put forth theories of classifying mental disorders as biological in nature and introduced a plan for more comprehensive form of psychiatry. This would set the stage for the DSM criteria currently used to classify mental disorders. At the time of this writing, the DSM-4 is currently in use as a diagnostic aid in classifying mental illness. Currently, the DSM-5 is being debated as to its strengths and weaknesses. There is also currently a grass-roots opposition to the DSM-5 which is fairly formidable.

At this point you're probably wondering why there is a chapter on psychiatry included in a book about nonconsensual experimentation with non-lethal weapons and directed energy. Allow me to enlighten you. From the beginning, the earliest research sub-projects included in the MKULTRA, MKSEARCH and similar projects were aimed at controlling the mind. Almost all of those sub-projects were directed by psychiatrists deriving their funding directly or indirectly from agencies like the CIA, NSA or DoD. Much of the experimentation was performed on non-consenting participants who were regarded as expendable in the name of national security. All of the psychiatrists exposed through FIOA and the Rockefeller Commission as to directing the research went on to be hailed as pioneers in their field and had glowing eulogies upon their deaths. All of this despite admissions of performing nonconsensual experimentation to congress and citing the interest of national security for their blatant disregard of the victims' rights. It is no mystery that the current victims of electromagnetic weapons research appear to be schizophrenic or suffering from delusional disorder. The technology was painstakingly designed to accurately mimic the symptoms that psychiatrists have determined fulfill the diagnosis of these respective disorders. As a matter of fact, psychiatrists at the community level have long been used as apologists for nonconsensual experimentation. Many of the victims of the early radiation and infectious agent experimentation were told they were delusional or schizophrenic once they started reporting symptoms and seeking medical assistance. Of course, decades later after many lives were ruined by illness and wrongful psychiatric diagnosis, the government did admit to nonconsensual experimentation and lame apologies were offered to survivors and their families. The last such apology was given by Secretary of State Hillary Clinton to the people of Guatemala for experimentation nonconsensually done on them by the NIH with syphilis contagion. Of course, the experimentation was done from 1946-1948 and the apology was given under duress from media exposure sixty years later in 2010 which is typical of our government. Current examples of very obvious experimentation such as these victims complaining of electronic harassment and Morgellon's Disease are likely in the same boat, awaiting an admission of guilt and an apology in 50-60 years. For those unfamiliar with Morgellon's Disease, it is being diagnosed in individuals breaking out with skin lesions from which non-human fibers, strands of other material are being removed. Despite a number of physicians sending biopsies from Morgellon's lesions to laboratories, verifying the presence of non-human matter, the excuse offered by the NIH and the CDC is that these victims suffer from delusional parasitosis. Remember, these are the same two agencies responsible for the Tuskegee syphilis study in the United States and the recently exposed syphilis study in Guatemala. I'm certain those victims were told that they were suffering from delusions at the same time as their experimentation as well. It appears as if the DSM-4 was intentionally set up to be able to sidetrack any truth about experimentation from being found out. The DSM-5 will be worse, not only for current victims of nonconsensual experimentation but for the population at large as well.

Upon its initial draft, the DSM-5 was mired in controversy. For the vast number of psychiatrists who support the new criteria an equally vast number thoroughly oppose it. Fundamentally, the biggest problem with the DSM-5 is that essentially no person, no matter how mentally stable, can escape getting some type of diagnosis or mental illness. The first Diagnostic and Statistical Manual of Mental Disorders (DSM) was published in 1952 in an attempt to standardize the criteria for diagnosing mental illness. It has been revised several times with the fifth revision (DSM-5) was published in May 2013. The codes in the DSM criteria also coincide with ICD billing codes, making it easier for psychiatrists to bill their services to third party payers. The American Psychiatric Association has been under fire for the DSM since its inception both for its content and the money generated by its publication. Each revision of the manual has included more previously normal behaviors as pathologic or worthy of diagnosis. The current revision or DSM-5 is no different. The publication of the DSM and its closely guarded copyrights nets the ADA over 5 million dollars a year. The money generated by the DSM and the influence that pharmaceutical companies have on its content have led to much controversy regarding its use.

The DSM-5 release in May 2013 has been surrounded in controversy since it began. The most controversial addendum to the DSM is the inclusion of psychosis risk syndrome also known as attenuated psychosis syndrome. This addendum was intended mainly for individuals hearing whispers in their heads, viewing objects as threatening or suffering from other subtly psychotic symptoms. It is amazingly coincidental that the APA, fully complicit in the MKULTRA mind experimentation projects, would find a way to include the 300,000 plus individuals hearing voices in their heads into diagnostic criteria in the DSM-5. For now, the psychosis risk syndrome has been dropped from the final publication. However, I can almost guarantee that it will be silently included as an addendum at a later date once the scrutiny is off the APA regarding the list of the DSM-5.

Dr. Allen Frances, M.D. served as Chair of the DSM-4 task force and is current professor emeritus of psychiatry at Duke University School of Medicine. He has been very outspoken against the DSM-5 due to the risk of it "medicalizing normality, resulting in a glut of unnecessary and harmful drug prescribing." In Psychology Today he listed the ten most harmful changes to the DSM-5 and recommends that they not be followed at all. 1) Disruptive Mood Dysregulation Disorder will turn childhood temper tantrums into a mental disorder with pharmacologic treatment recommended. It will exacerbate the already excessive and inappropriate use of medication in young children. This decision was based upon research from only one group. 2) Normal grief will become Major Depressive Disorder thus making our normal and necessary emotional reactions to the loss of a loved one a treatable condition. Under this change grief will be treated with pills and medical interventions rather than family consolation and pastoral care. 3) The forgetfulness of old age will now be misdiagnosed as Minor Neurocognitive Disorder, creating a huge false positive population of people who have no risk of dementia. 4) The diagnosis of Adult Attention Deficit Disorder will be exacerbated leading to a further widespread misuse of stimulant medications contributing to the already large illegal secondary market in diverted stimulants. 5) Excessive eating 12 times within a 3 month period is no longer a manifestation of the easy availability of great food. According to the DSM-5 it is a psychiatric illness called Binge Eating Disorder. 6) The new definition of Autism in the DSM-5 will result in lower rates of diagnosis. According to the DSM-5 work group it will decrease by 10 percent; however, outside research groups are estimating a 50 percent reduction in the diagnosis. 7) First time substance abusers will be lumped in definitionally with hard-core addicts despite their very different treatment needs and prognosis. 8) The DSM-5 has created a slippery slope by introducing the concept of behavioral addictions that eventually can spread to make a mental disorder out of everything we like to do a lot. The over diagnosis of internet and sex addiction will undoubtedly contribute to lucrative treatment progress to exploit these new markets. 9) The DSM-5 obscures the already fuzzy boundary between Generalized Anxiety Disorder and the worries of everyday life. This will increase the number of people inappropriately prescribed addictive anti-anxiety medications. 10) The DSM-5 opens the gate further to the already existing problem of the misdiagnosis of PTSD in forensic settings.

According to Dr. Frances, people with real psychiatric problems that can be reliably diagnosed and effectively treated are already badly shortchanged. The DSM-5 will make this worse by diverting attention and scare resources away from the legitimately ill and toward people with the everyday problems of life who will be harmed, not helped, when they are mislabeled as mentally ill. Such is currently the case of victims of nonconsensual experimentation in this country. Almost all of the victims that have complained of electronic harassment have eventually been seen by a psychiatrist who is more apt to "medicalize" them into the confines of the DSM-4 rather than investigate their claims of experimentation. A cursory Google search would easily lead them into the dark world of organized stalking and electronic harassment. The sheer matter of victims' testimonies, websites, information sites and humanitarian organizations directed to addressing electronic harassment should steer an ethical psychiatrist into seeing the reality of this issue. However, because the practice of psychiatry is pharmaco-financially driven, the victim is found within the parameters of the DSM-4, soon to be DSM-5, and placed in treatment. Since most victims are in their late 30's to 50's, with no history of psychiatric illness, they are usually spared the diagnosis of schizophrenia in favor of delusional disorder of the non-bizarre type. Delusional Disorder is divided into the subtypes of bizarre or non-bizarre, and further broken down to persecutory, grandiose, jealous, erotomanic, and somatic. Non-bizarre means that the victims' complaints are plausible, just not in their case. The victim is then placed on psychotropic drugs that will not help, and financially strapped with $300 an hour psychiatric visits during which their doctor will try to convince them of their delusional status, while their perpetrators continually whisper in their ears, "we told you so."

What the reader should glean from my rant on psychiatry is this: In medical school one can spot the individuals destined for psychiatry on day one. For the most part they are strange individuals, often searching for self-help, and remain strange individuals throughout their career as physicians focused on what they see as the more intellectual practice of medicine. Many choose psychiatry out of a fear of treating patients or seeing their blood, sputum, urine, or feces that those of us in real fields of medicine must deal with on a daily basis. Psychiatry, unlike all other fields of medicine, has absolutely no basis in hard science. Since there is no lab test or MRI to diagnosis "crazy", clusters of behaviors are corralled into groups and given big medical names to simulate a diagnosis, mostly for medical billing purposes. Billing is a large part of psychiatry! Most psychiatrists will not take insurance and charge an average of about $300 per hour. Hence, the true mentally ill, the homeless, are left untreated in favor of treating the people with average life stresses with pharmaceutical drugs that generate billions of dollars to fund even more psychiatric residency programs. One can see from the changes proposed in the DSM-5 that the ultimate goal of the APA is to medicate every man, woman, and child on the continent eventually. That fact shouldn't be too difficult to understand since I've illustrated the fact that the APA has been deeply involved with the CIA for quite some time. Their recommendations have altered society for the worse and have resulted in the proliferation of pharmaceuticals whose side effects far outweigh their efficacy. Moreover, psychiatry has been the punitive arm of most DoD, federal, state and local government agencies who have learned that they can discredit and marginalize whistle-blowers very easily with psychiatrists who are paid to give an individual a damning diagnosis. If you are a victim of electronic harassment, or have been mandated to see a psychiatrist for any reason for that matter, you must remember that the doctor behind the desk may not be your enemy but he is also not looking out for your best interest. Apart from hearing a bunch of impressive medical terms for mental illness, none of which are based on scientific evidence, the janitor cleaning his office at the end of the day knows as much about the human mind as he does.

In closing, as a medical student I remember seeing a video skit of a physician doing a parody of the infamous General Patten speech in front of the American Flag. He changed the famous closing line to read as follows: "When you're old and gray, sitting on your front porch, sipping your mint julep with your grandson on your knee, he may ask, "Grandpa what did you do in the Great War on disease?" You sure as hell don't want to have to say," well....I did psychotherapy."

CHAPTER 10

Rise of the Sociocracy

"For even when we were with you, this we commanded you
that, if any would not work, neither should he eat."
                                        –2 Thessalonians 3:10

For some time Biblical scholars and liberal proponents of socialism have argued back and forth over the Biblical interpretation of economics. They are dramatically over thinking the issue. God is a capitalist and the Bible teaches the virtues of a free market economy. The verse above from 2 Thessalonians clearly extolls the virtue of hard work and providing for one's self. Moreover, one of the Ten Commandments, "Thou shalt not steal" clearly advocates the individual's right to private property. Ironically, Socialists always turned to quotes from the Bible regarding charity for the poor in their argument for Socialism being the basis of the Bible. True, the Bible does emphasize charitable giving to help the poor. Most Christian churches have charitable programs in place that utilize donations for outreach to the impoverished for food, medical aid, dental aid and other necessities. The funding comes from donations from parishioners who feel God has blessed them and choose to share their wealth as a sharing of God's blessing with those less fortunate than themselves. Socialism on the other hand, advocates helping the poor by stealing from the wealthy. This is evident in the progressive tax system that is currently in place in the United States. One of our founding fathers in the United States, Benjamin Franklin, best summarized how poverty should be handled. "I think the best way of doing good to the poor, is not making them easy in poverty, but leading or driving them out of it." Unfortunately, the rational inclination of most human beings is to fulfill one's lowest expectation of them. Too many people have found it more comfortable to subsist at a level slightly above poverty, as provided by the government, than to seek a gainful living where they are paid for their labor. The time has now come where the number of people deriving their existence from the government exceeds the number of working people financially contributing to the system. Democracy ends and Socialism begins at this point. Unfortunately, that time is now.

So what does all this have to do with electronic harassment, you are probably asking. This is where we delve into the very complex reason of why it's happening and to what end the goal of all the suffering is directed. History has shown us that Marxist socialism does not work on a grand scale. In small groups, where each individual contributes and the resources are divided equally among the workers, it does seem to appear advantageous. However, at a national level it fails miserably for two reasons. First, the national wealth flows upward into government hands where government officials controlling the supposed redistribution of wealth become corrupt as only human nature can dictate. Second, redistribution of wealth is at the expense of the wealthy and working class, thus creating an exponentially larger impoverished class of citizens. Indeed, observations of other socialist countries demonstrate the fact that poor stay poor, the working class becomes poor and those in government live opulently. This fact should be familiar to you since United States Congress members have an annual salary of around $175,000 per year while the average American worker is $39,416 per year. Socialism sounds great in theory, especially to the less privileged, but the discrepancy of wealth secondary to confiscating wealth from the financially successful creates class warfare that never goes away. Hence, we see domestic struggles in socialist countries having to constantly repress groups wanting change. Nonetheless, liberals continue to push for a more socialistic version of government in the United States under the guise of "leveling the playing field" through social engineering. Not one of them will use the term Marxism or Socialism; it's all about "social engineering," "redistribution of wealth," or "socio-financial reform." All of the previous are the new key words for socialism. Unfortunately, Democrats and Republicans alike have members pushing this agenda. Agenda 21, a United Nations program, is the ultimate experiment in Socialism with our current State Department solidly in support of its tenets. Agenda 21 outlines the stepwise process by which the industrialized nations will surrender their sovereignty to a one world government made up of elite members of the United Nations. They realized years ago that military actions and taxes cannot control the entire population. The technology being used experimentally at this time in cases of electronic harassment may one day be used to control a global population.

That day got exponentially closer on November 4, 2008 with the election of Barack Hussein Obama to the presidency of the United States. Many victims of electronic harassment that I've spoken with have a strong hatred for former President Bush and his vice president, Dick Cheney. They place a large amount of the blame on the Bush Administration for their targeting, mostly because of his passing of the Patriot Act which does deeply infringe upon our right to privacy. However, this type of experimentation started in the 1960's, long before Bush ever thought about running for President. The technology behind electronic harassment has been refined over decades as advances in technology have made it easier and easier to deploy. President Obama, promising governmental transparency, has had the most opaque State Department we have ever had. Many victims of electronic harassment felt certain that the promises of transparency would translate into disclosure of the technology being used against them and their torture would cease upon his election. The Obama administration has done nothing about nonconsensual experimentation and appears to be using electromagnetic technology at an accelerated rate far beyond that of prior administrations. Despite thousands of testimonials and petitions directed toward the Obama Administration regarding electronic harassment, no action has been taken. Even worse, he appointed a Bioethics Commission to research the possibility of nonconsensual experimentation that may be ongoing in the United States or abroad. I spoke at the first Bioethics Commission meeting and submitted well written documents from other physicians dealing with victims of electromagnetic experimentation. Hundreds of victims themselves appeared at the public forums voicing their complaints directly to his appointed board. In the end, his board appointed apologists denied any substantial evidence of nonconsensual experimentation in the face of an overwhelming amount of evidence to the contrary. As a matter of fact, victims of electronic harassment were specifically asked not to show up to their later meetings and several victims were forcibly removed from the proceedings before they could have their voices heard. Is this the transparency we were promised?

2012 saw the same reelection of President Obama and the continued rise of sociocracy. I use the term sociocracy to describe the unique form of socialism currently being forced upon the

American people. Most strict socialist countries do not have elections; if they do, they are strictly for appearance sake and the same leaders are continually elected. Chavez in Venezuela and Putin in Russia are fairly good examples of this. However, in the United States we still hold elections and have the illusion of being able to make a choice between two or three different ideologies with regard to the candidates and their respective parties. In reality, it doesn't seem to matter who is elected; the outcome will likely be the same. Of course, there are exceptions, but the lifelong professional politicians on both sides are looking for control of the population through excessive government and unusual regulations resulting in the dismantling of our freedoms and liberties. The Obama Administration has set the gold standard for pushing through regulatory legislation that will prove to be detrimental to the citizens of the United States. Moreover, he has surrounded himself with lifelong liberal democratic senators who are also on board with his socialist agenda.

Upon Obama's election in 2008, he immediately appointed a series of Czars to direct various elements of government. These appointees were placed into positions of power without congressional vetting or any type of oversight other than media vetting. For some time now the mainstream media has been largely liberal and proponents of the growing sociocracy, so the history of these newly appointed Czars was quite sugar-coated. A short list of the more troubling Czars that he appointed is as follows:

    1) Cass Sunstein, Regulatory Czar: Believes free speech should be limited, believes the Federal Government should fund abortion with tax dollars, wrote that the government should have the right to harvest organs from those terminally ill with no prospect of life.

    2) John Holdren, Science Czar: Believes that forced

abortion and mass sterilization is needed to save the planet. Liberals dispute his position on eugenics but he co-authored a book entitled Ecoscience: Population, Resources, and Environment in 1977 putting forth plans for eugenics programs sponsored by the government.

3) Van Jones, Green Jobs Czar: Well-known member of STORM, a group that is pro-Marxist and communist.

4) R. Gil Kerlikowske, Drug Czar: Lobbyist for restrictive gun laws and supports legalization of all drugs.

5) Carol Browner, Climate Czar: She is a member of Socialist International and is a proponent of global government.

6) Donald Berwick, Health Czar: Admits that redistribution of health care means rationing health care.

7) John O Brennen, Terrorism Czar: Long history with the CIA and was Station Chief in Saudi Arabia. FBI sources have reported that he converted to Islam while in Saudi Arabia. He was appointed CIA Director in 2013 amid much controversy.

These are just a sample of some of Obama's appointed Czars. The list is extensive and most have radical liberal agendas that, of course, fall in line with President Obama's himself. The American public has long been duped into thinking that the Democratic Party is the party looking out for the common people and their welfare. The Republican Party had long been vilified, especially after passage of the Patriot Act under President Bush, as the party seeking control of the public. I think as you read more it will be clear that the liberal, democratic agenda is more disturbing than anything the Republicans have ever passed. As a matter of fact, the only legislators that have ever been willing to sit and talk to me about nonconsensual experimentation in this country have been Republicans. I know for a fact that

Congresswomen Feinstein and Pelosi, both from California, have received numerous letters from their constituents complaining of electronic harassment. Neither Congresswoman has responded to request for dialogue regarding this topic nor have they responded to letters of complaints from victims in their home state of California which has had the highest number of complaints. It should be evident that there is an ethical void in Washington D.C. and as long as we keep electing to office the most immoral among us, we will not see change for the better.

At the time of this writing we are well into the second term of the Obama presidency. The rise of sociocracy is more evident now that during his first term when the initial groundwork was put into place. The appointment of his Czars should've heeded us enough warning not to re-elect him but these warnings were ignored as the public was once again enamored with his promises. Never mind that none of his promises made during the first campaign ever came to fruition. During the first campaign he promised government transparency. There have been more backroom deals and unvetted appointments than in any prior administration to date. He also promised to lessen the national deficit, close Guantanamo Prison, end the war in Afghanistan and decrease taxes. To date, none of his promises have been fulfilled. However, he has accomplished putting this country in the worst debt it has ever known. Under Obama the national debt has grown by 6 trillion dollars, the largest increase under any president in American history. He forced Obama Care through Congress by placing the bill in committees with only several days for legislators to try and read the extensive bill before voting on it. It was signed into law without anyone really knowing what was actually in it. As Nancy Pelosi was quoted, "we have to pass it to know what's in it." We now know a little bit about what's in it. It will raise taxes on the middle class, cost more than originally projected, result in the loss of coverage to many Americans, cause a shortage of physicians and result in massive job losses due to the provision that forces employers to provide insurance to full time employees. As a physician, I admit that our healthcare system in the United States has been mediocre; however, Obama Care is a costly and destructive alternative.

At the time of this writing we have seen severe upheaval across the globe. Several European countries have seen economic collapse necessitating them to turn to the International Monetary Fund for financial aid. In exchange for bail-out finances, those countries in need must turn over a percentage of control to the IMF. Cyprus was bailed out financially by the European Union who ordered the government of Cyprus to confiscate a percentage of the wealth of the populace by taking money out of their checking and savings accounts. News of this plan was leaked out through the media and a run on the banks occurred with people pulling their cash out of their bank accounts. The economy in the United States has been artificially bolstered with government, tax funded bail-outs of the banking system in continuation with the Federal Reserve printing more money to accommodate demand. Economists predict that eventually the over-printing of money and uncontrollable government spending will eventually lead to an economic collapse here as the dollar becomes more devalued and severe inflation takes hold. There are no safeguards in place in the United States preventing the government from confiscating personal accounts in a time of crisis as happened in Cyprus. As a matter of fact, it has happened here before with the gold confiscation executive order in 1933 which prevented private citizens from owning gold from 1933-1974. Under the current Obama Administration I could easily see confiscation happening again. Essentially it's already happening with increased corporate taxation, increased tax on the middle and upper classes, limits on the amount one can put in an IRA, carbon emissions tax and a pending Federal sales tax on internet transactions.

The Obama regime, touting itself as the most transparent state department in history, has proven itself to be the most opaque our country has ever seen. As I write, the news on both conservative and liberal channels is attacking the Obama administration on their major fronts. First, on the anniversary of the 911 attack on the World Trade Center Towers, the United States Consulate was attacked in Benghazi, Libya. The attack occurred between 11pm on September 11th and lasted through 2am on September 12, 2012. The Consulate was attacked by a group called Ansar Al-Sharia, an offshoot of Al-Qaeda who used RPG's, hand grenades, mortars, and anti-aircraft machine guns to perpetrate the attack. Ambassador Chris Stevens was abducted, attacked, sodomized, and murdered while Tyrone Woods, Sean Smith, and Glen Doherty were killed in their attempt to defend the compound. A steady live stream of drone video was sent to the State Department as well as phone calls and emails stating that the consulate was under terrorist attack. Military reinforcements to assist the beleaguered were told to stand down and not proceed to Benghazi. For months after the attack, Ambassador Susan Rice, Secretary of State Hillary Clinton, and President Obama repeatedly blamed an anti-Islamic video for the attack in front of all of the major press outlets. The attempted cover-up of the attack at Benghazi resulted in congressional hearings during which insiders present at the attack gave testimony in direct conflict with the Obama Administration's reasoning for the attack. These hearings are currently ongoing and along with two other scandals have kept Jay Karney, press secretary for the Obama Administration, busy finding novel ways to present this administration's lies to the public.

The second scandal involves the IRS, the single most

powerful entity in our government holding the capability to ruin both corporations and individuals. Recently it has come to light that the IRS has been specifically targeting conservative organizations and individuals outspoken against the government, specifically the Obama Administration. The San Antonio, Texas Tea Party and a Houston group called True the Vote were two local non-profit organizations targeted. In addition to IRS audits, Catherine Engelbrecht, the founder of Houston's True the Vote, was also targeted by the FBI, OSHA, BATF and the EPA. For those unfamiliar with True the Vote, it is a non-partisan, non-profit organization that monitors polling stations for fraud. However, despite its non-partisan nature, the Democratic Party of Texas and ACORN have both also filed lawsuits against True the Vote. Of course, President Obama claims he didn't know of the IRS targeting until he saw it on the news and accepted Steven Miller's resignation as head of the IRS. Currently, Mr. Miller is being defiant in the face of congressional hearings, just as Hillary Clinton was regarding Benghazi. The person in charge of handling non-profit applications with the IRS during its alleged targeting of conservative organizations was Sarah Hall Ingram. Incidentally, before resigning Steven Miller promoted her to the Administrative position of the IRS overseeing Obama Care. There will be many more questions presented over time regarding this IRS scandal as more and more individuals come forward with their stories of targeting. Many victims of nonconsensual experimentation that have become politically outspoken have suffered IRS targeting after starting web pages or blogs regarding their torture. Thirdly, another scandal facing the Obama Administration and the Department of Justice under Attorney General Eric Holder is the seizure of phone records from Associated Press offices, reporters' office phones, and cell phones. For the most part, the Associated Press typically has a liberal spin on what they report and usually tailor their stories to reflect positively on the Obama Administration. Unfortunately, this did not protect them from the peering eyes of a government running amuck. The Chief Executive of the Associated Press, Gary Pruitt, said that the secret seizure of two months of its phone records was unconstitutional and diminished journalist's capacity to report on the government. Of course, the Obama Administration is denying that it knew anything about the seizure of reporters' phone records. Although, not long after the news of the phone records seizure broke, a Fox News reporter was indicted for being a co-conspirator in a security leak case he reported on. Reporter James Rosen received a subpoena for his emails and phone records after FBI agent Reginald Reyes described him as a co-conspirator for doing a standard journalism job regarding the story. This is currently a growing scandal and has re-ignited congressional requests for Attorney General Holder's resignation from the Department of Justice which began after his "Fast and Furious" gun scandal came to light. In an effort to make gun control more palatable to the American public, Holder had straw purchases of assault weapons delivered to drug cartels in Mexico in the hope that they would be tracked back to American gun sellers in the United States upon confiscation. Obama has long opined that the Cartels are accessing assault weapons from American gun dealers in Texas, New Mexico and Arizona. "Fast and Furious" was supposed to make this statement appear true to the American voting public. The operation backfired and congressional attempts at investigating it have been thwarted by the Department of Justice despite the deaths of two Border Patrol agents because of it. Moreover, in May 2013, in a speech delivered in Mexico, Obama is still blaming American gun dealers for arming the drug cartels.

The main reason for including this chapter in the book was

to contradict many of the theories about former President Bush and Vice President Cheney as the impetus behind electronic harassment. A vast majority of targeted individuals voted for Obama in both elections in hope of the terms that he promised. The Obama Administration has shown themselves to be the least transparent of any administration this country has ever seen. Their entire agenda appears to be catapulting the United States into a sociocracy and away from a democratic republic as the Constitution intended. Under the last five years of the Obama administration we have seen obedience to detrimental United Nations recommendations, social engineering, re-distribution of wealth, nationalization of financial institutions, governmental control of private industry, excess taxation, the worst growing national debt in history and governmental control over health care. Unfortunately, it appears as though the Democratic Party, which has always leaned left, has been successfully hijacked by socialists looking for help to fulfill the United Nations dream of being a One World Government. While many of the changes already made to our society are probably irreversible, four more years of another Democratic State Department following Obama's second term will probably result in the worst surveillance state in the United States that the world has ever known. The American public needs to think long and hard about who they elect to Federal office in the upcoming elections. If we continue to elect the most uninformed and unethical among us to positions of power, we will exponentially hasten our own enslavement to a government bent on controlling us. At last, mainstream media is finally recognizing the agenda of control occurring within the Government; however they are oblivious to the modalities being used to achieve it.

CHAPTER 11
Surveillance State

"For nothing is secret, that shall not be made manifest; neither anything hid, that shall not be known and come abroad."

–Luke 8:17

As I sit and write this chapter I can clearly see that the summer of 2013 will clearly be known in the future as the summer of our discontent. Proudly, we elected our first African American President to symbolize our rise above our racist past, believing wholeheartedly his promises of change and transparency in government. White guilt, black pride and a politically ignorant public brought the least qualified person to the White House that our nation has ever seen. Barack Obama and his band of corrupt Chicago cronies hoodwinked the people not once, but twice in his election to the Presidency of the United States. His promises of government transparency and protection of individual privacy was campaign rhetoric at best and well planned lies at worst. The summer of 2013 would see his administration embroiled in at least five controversial scandals that even the most liberal media outlets could not ignore. The year 2013 ushered in a new era when topics previously reserved for alternative news outlets of conspiracy theory websites suddenly appeared in newspapers, websites and television news shows of the mainstream media.

As congressional hearings about Operation Fast and Furious, the IRS targeting enemies of the Democratic Party, the Benghazi attack and Department of Justice seizure of press phone records are ongoing; another bombshell is dropped by the Guardian news outlet in the U.K. Reporter Glenn Greenwald, citing insider information from a whistleblower, exposes a vast and corrupt system of surveillance by the NSA in the United States and abroad. Edward Snowden, a twenty-nine year old who has subcontracted by the NSA and CIA through private companies like Booze Allen Hamilton and Dell, decided it was his moral obligation to expose the extent of full spectrum surveillance happening within the NSA. According to Snowden, "my sole motive is to inform the public as to that which is done in their name and that which is done against them." He is currently in hiding, as much as one can hide, in Hong Kong awaiting further extradition proceedings or an attempted CIA rendition. Mr. Snowden was offered asylum in Russia prior to the release of this book. Mr. Snowden thought about coming forward with information much earlier but with the election of Barack Obama, he believed the promises that privacy reforms would be enacted and held back from any exposure. After witnessing the Obama Administration prosecute whistleblowers at a historically unprecedented rate, he decided to come forward. One may view President Bush as having snapped the football to the holder when he passed the Patriot Act, President Obama kicked it hard and fast through the upright.

I'm really shocked that the mainstream media has reacted with such shock that the NSA is surveilling its own citizens with such full spectrum surveillance. Targeted individuals have known this for quite some time, collecting into human rights organizations and petitioning their respective congress people as well as the responsible agencies for exposure. While pseudonyms like "Boundless Informant", the tool for cataloging data obtained by the NSA and "Prism", the program used to tap into user data of Apple, Google and Facebook are recent terms we've known about for some time. The current debacle within the NSA involves real time collection of cell phone data from Verizon; but don't think you're safe with AT&T. Reporter James Bamford, in his book entitled "The Shadow Factory" that was published in 2008, described in detail how AT&T allowed the NSA to install surveillance equipment attached to its fiber optic splitting system at 611 Folsom Street in San Francisco. As far back as 2006, citing insider information, I repeatedly mentioned the connections between Facebook, Google and In-Q-Tel. In-Q-Tel is a non-profit venture capital firm formed by the CIA in 1999 tasked with delivering technology to the intelligence community. The biggest hoax ever perpetuated on the public was fostering their dependence on Google and Facebook, two of the most powerful data mining tools ever conceived by the Government and passed off as completely private sector entities.

Alarmingly, the usual suspects have come to the defense of the NSA, citing national security and the war on terrorism as justification for full spectrum surveillance on the public. Mike Rogers, Chairman of the House Intelligence Committee, Diane Feinstein, Senate Intelligence Committee Chair, and President Obama have all come to the defense of the NSA and called for Snowden's prosecution for leaking information. The mainstream media is somewhat mixed on perception of Snowden, some following Obama's lead in calling him a traitor, others viewing him as a patriotic hero. Either way, the smear campaign has begun with government officials questioning the validity of his claims. They are mostly citing his lack of formal education as the determining factor about the extent of his true knowledge of these surveillance programs. However, this is meant to mislead the public. In actuality, intelligence agencies actively seek out savant loners with limited family connections as agents, especially if they have exceptional, self-taught computer skills. The other misleading comment that government officials have made regarding Snowden's exposure is that it puts the US at greater risk for terrorist attack by letting terrorists know how our surveillance operates. Any terrorist worth his salt is already well aware of surveillance methods. For instance, Terror Networks in Afghanistan pass information between individuals using written notes carried by runners who are mostly children. Their Jihadist websites are mostly filled with diversional information so as not to have a digital trail. Our surveillance methods have prevented few, if any, terrorist attacks including the latest Boston Marathon bombing, despite a Russian warning about the two brothers who perpetrated it. Obviously, the counter surveillance apparatus within the United States Government is meant to watch us, not protect us or prevent any type of terrorist attack. I believe that the Prism and Boundless Informant programs are intimately linked to the electronic harassment and experimentation being currently perpetrated on the public. As more information is leaked, we will see eventually that Prism and Boundless Informant are merely the surveillance tentacles of a larger hydra that is more akin to a weapon system rather than tools for solely observing our actions.

The breaking news about the NSA comes as no surprise to the many victims of electronic harassment; they've been under full spectrum surveillance for a full decade or longer in many cases. Reports of email tampering, computer hacking, mail tampering, and cell phone spoofing are fairly standard complaints among the myriad of other intrusions that targeted individuals describe. The amount of time, energy and money that the United States Government has invested in novel ways to digitally track the citizens of the United States is mind boggling. In the short time between the publishing of my first book, A New Breed, and this one, there have been countless new developments aimed at perfecting the surveillance state. Some of these include: 1) the inclusion of facial recognition software on Facebook. 2) Border Patrol kiosks that use voice pattern software to monitor pitch and quality along with infrared cameras that monitor the eye movement and pupil dilatation to detect liars. 3) The current research on deep sea drones used for intelligence, surveillance and reconnaissance in contested waters called the Upward Falling Payloads Program. 4) the fielding of the Cognitive Technology Threat Warning System (CT_2WS) that are binoculars that function off of the soldiers brainwaves to assess threat detection. The EEG interactive binoculars sense the P-300 brainwave signal involved in stimulus evaluation and categorization before the soldier has even processed the situation. 5) NSA ability to lock into surveillance cameras in stores, in computers and in phones using Remote Administration Tools (RATs) allowing your home electronic devices to be used as spy tools. 6) The use of millimeter wave sensors in airports allowing TSA agents to see passengers' naked bodies as they pass through security. The Fraunhofer radar unit that miniaturized millimeter wave scanners down to the size of a cigarette box. 7) The FBI admission of using domestic drones in a recent comment by FBI Director Robert Mueller during his congressional hearing. 8) The miniaturization and proliferation of GPS technology in our vehicles, laptop computers and cell phones. 9) The inclusion of RFID tags in nearly all of our household goods and apparel. 10) Smart meters for home electrical wiring which can be used for surveillance. According to the ACLU, Californians big three utilities have already been allowing government agencies to acquire data from certain meters. 11) Smart Dust formulated to scatter broadly around large areas of the country that will allow tracking of population movement. 12) Very recent unleashing of Al Sight technology by BRS Labs. Al Sight is a computer program that monitors thousands of security cameras simultaneously and identifies abnormal behavior. According to BRS President, John Frazzini, it gives law enforcement the ability to "identify unusual behavioral activity that could lead to pre-crime investigation." It is in current use in San Diego, California. 13) Extensive ongoing research on Brain machine Interfaces (BMI) where the human brain itself will be intentionally linked to computer central systems. 14) Ongoing DNA data basing through the nonconsensual testing of every newborn for Phenylketonuria with a heel stick for a blood sample. In 30 states the baby's DNA is considered property of the state. The FBI DNA database called CODIS was intended only for sex offenders but was recently expanded to include DNA samples from almost any criminal offender.

The previous examples of some of the new cutting edge surveillance tools are merely the droplets of water lightly touching down on the tip of the iceberg. An entire encyclopedia of novel surveillance technology could be written, which would need to be revised and updated on a daily basis. The latest topics in surveillance and control currently reside within the neurosciences. We lost our privacy, or expectation of privacy, in our cell phone calls, text messages, and emails long ago. Despite the reaction of the press to the current NSA exposure of mass surveillance, most of us have known it's been going on since at least 2006. However, the human mind is the philosopher's stone to the alphabet agencies that wish to control us. Since the late 1950's every government agency you may be able to think of, and some you've never heard of, has spent millions of dollars trying to turn lead into gold with regard to unlocking the secrets of the brain. As a matter of fact, in April 2013, President Obama approved 100 million dollars to be spent on his BRAIN Initiative project which is designed to map the inner workings of the human brain. BRAIN, or brain research through advancing innovative neurotechnologies, is allegedly tasked with recording the activities of individual cells and neurons within the brain. According to Obama, "Our scientists are mapping the human brain to unlock the answers of Alzheimer's." Of course the project is headed up by DARPA along with the National Institutes of Health and the National Science Foundation. Their private sector partners will be The Allen Institute for Brain Science, Howard Hughes Medical Institute, The Kavli Foundation and the Salk Institute for Biologic Studies. I will be as brave to state that we will never see any medically worthwhile results come from this project, but rather see more novel neurologic weapons arise.

The government agencies heading up the project might have all been involved in nonconsensual experimentation at one time or another before. DARPA has long been at the forefront of emerging weapon technologies as well. The Allen Institute for Brain Science was founded in 2003 in Seattle as a Seattle based non-profit medical research organization founded by Microsoft Executive Paul Allen. Howard Hughes Medical Institute was mired in controversy in 2002 when Don C. Wiley, a DNA researcher, was found dead under mysterious circumstances along with six other world-class microbiologists that same year. The Kavli Foundation specializes in neuroscience research along with astrophysics, neuroscience, and theoretical physics. The Salk Institute gained some unwanted notoriety in 2012 when it came to light that Aurora, Colorado shooter James Holms had interned at the Salk Institute. Interested in mind control, Holms had allegedly designed a computer program to alter mental states using flicker rates while at Salk. Flicker rate manipulation has long been used in video to induce certain mental states. Many websites are claiming that James Holmes was a mind control victim. Nevertheless, the Obama BRAIN

Initiative is completely being handled by organizations with links to weapons technology which makes me very suspect of its proposed medical contributions.

As you can see the surveillance state in the United States is alive and well and expanding at an exponential rate. The governing elite are no longer content to govern and are seeking the ability to totally control the population. Complete control of the media along with full spectrum surveillance has led the United States public down the primrose path to total and complete ignorance about any of the true agendas of our own elected government. If one looks at our current situation logically, we are already controlled. The only information we are allowed to incorporate into our decision making processes is that which the major media is allowed to feed us. Every now and again a major media source will slip and accidently incorporate something truthful into a story but it is usually whitewashed or later disappears completely from public view. All the while our text messages, cell phones, and emails are being monitored to distinguish between those who are continuing to exhibit self-decision and those who are regurgitating the propaganda. It has become almost impossible to make an informed decision about anything in the United States based upon the information we are allowed to know. Moreover, in addition to the lack of honest information in the major media, we also have to cipher through governmental diversion. The Obama Administration has mastered this cornerstone tradecraft of subterfuge. For example, as the Obama Administration became more and more mired in scandal, to the point where even the press couldn't keep ignoring it, all of a sudden Syria became an immediate problem. Democrats and some Republicans began beating the war drums for military action in Syria in the name of human rights. The press was more than willing to cover possible military action in

Syria, the George Zimmerman trial, or any available celebrity antics rather than address NSA surveillance, IRS targeting, immigration reform, or the healthcare debacle. The Obama Administration has helped the United Nations destabilize several Arab countries that were under relatively good control by the United States. The Assad regime in Syria is brutal, but the rebels are Al-Qaeda based and have already expressed their hatred for the United States. It would be in our best interest to allow those two groups to kill each other for as long as they would like to without interjection from the United States. This is a feeling shared by many of my contacts within military intelligence circles as well.

The year 2013 also saw the use of RFID badges used in the public schools for the first time. Unfortunately, this occurred in my hometown of San Antonio, Texas. Northside Independent School District began issuing school ID's embedded with RFID tracking chips which monitor their student's movements. Allegedly, the chip only allows them to be tracked while on school property and is an attempt to secure Federal funding which is based on attendance. A Federal judge ruled that the school was permitted to expel a student for refusing to wear their tag. One student, 15 year old Andrea Hernandez and her family fought the ruling on the religious grounds that it violated their beliefs. Her family sees the RFID tag as the "Mark of the Beast" from Revelations in the Bible. The court ruled against the girl's religious objections as she was mostly ridiculed for her beliefs by the press. This is unfortunate because surveillance and control do not get forced on us overnight, but rather get assembled like a jigsaw puzzle, one piece at a time until the puzzle is complete. School RFID for tracking students is but one piece. In another public school in Pennsylvania, the students were issued laptops for school use. What the Lower Merion School District failed to tell the students was that the camera on the laptop could be remotely accessed by school administrators. In addition to monitoring their emails, they also took still shots of students in their bedrooms using the remote control function of the laptop cameras. The school admitted that they had the software for covertly activating the cameras but denied any wrongdoing. It's bad enough that we have allowed public schools to dumb-down our children with federally mandated curriculum, but now they are tracking them and spying on them? As a society we should be outraged and calling for it to end, but the media always seems to find a believable reason to convince the public that it needs to continue. The generation of children currently in high school and college has no hope of ever enjoying the privacy that those of us over 40 years of age once enjoyed. They have had a digital footprint ever since starting school; their DNA data based and have been lured in by social media sites. Today's youth willingly share their personal information with whatever agency happens to be monitoring popular sites such as Twitter and Facebook. The surveillance state has made it increasingly easy for the government to pursue its divide and conquer program with the American public. As long as the government controls the major media while simultaneously monitoring every aspect of the public sector's private information, it will always know what buttons to push and when to get a desired effect. Usually the effect they are looking for is one that divides or polarizes the public. Every government fears a unified populace. People are much easier to control when you have them turning on each other in one fashion or another. The Obama Administration has been very successful at creating a diversion on almost every level. Through major media and social media this administration has intentionally fanned the flames between gay and straight, men and women, poor and wealthy, immigrants and citizens and most recently blacks and whites. As I mentioned earlier, the George Zimmerman trial has been an excellent diversion for CNN and MSNBC to use as an excuse for not covering more pressing issues currently facing our society. However, the government involvement in that trial is even more troubling than the crime, or the media coverage. The instant that the Trayvon Martin shooting appeared to be a white on black crime the Obama Administration and the Department of Justice was there to fan the flames in hopes of furthering racial division. Never mind the fact that the shooter was actually Hispanic, he has a white last name so the wheels began to spin at the DOJ. What you didn't hear in the major media was that initially there was no plan to charge George Zimmerman with any crime. Pressure from the DOJ is what brought about the trial and money from the DOJ helped fund the rallies and paid for transporting students from other areas to attend the rallies in support of Trayvon Martin. Despite the FBI having already investigated the shooting and deemed it not to be racially motivated, the DOJ is still making plans to pursue Zimmerman with criminal civil rights charges. On July 13, 2013 a Florida jury did find George Zimmerman "not guilty" of murder or manslaughter, and as expected some rioting did occur in Oakland with less violent protests in New York and San Francisco. The shooting was a tragic event that occurred between two men who both made bad decisions that night but was not racially motivated. However, I use this as a current example of how the government will use its resources and media bias to make it appear as something it's not to facilitate division. This is the same tactic that has been used for decades in third world countries to incite rebellions and sometimes revolutions. However, to the unsavvy public that sees tremendous demonstrations whether they are regarding gay rights, environmental issues, gun control or racial issues, it is never clarified for the public watching them on the news that many of the demonstrators are paid participants. In all demonstrations where the government is behind an agenda, the protestors are merely paid performers fulfilling their federally funded Shakespearean role of making the public believe as the government wants it to believe.

For the first time in human existence surveillance technology has reached the point where population trends, individual desires and dislikes, thoughts and dreams, societal values and any fears that may be reduced to statistics that can be manipulated. The government now controls the flow of information into the system, determines how we dispense it among us, and can predictably achieve the outcomes they desire from the initial information that was released. If an individual dares to question the source of the information they will know that as well and can take action against that individual through any one of a myriad of control systems. For example, when the IRS was found guilty of targeting conservative based 401C organizations, it was discovered that they had used keywords to determine the groups to target. Any group that used the keywords "constitution", "tea party", "conservative", or "patriot" in their application were targeted for further investigation by not only the IRS but many other Federal organizations. The hope was that many, if not all of the organizations would find the uphill battle too difficult to fight and would just dissolve. Our government fears a unified population in this country that will one day come to expect morality and proper ethical behavior among its leaders. Our current government wants to maintain and expand the control mechanisms that it has painstakingly put in place under the guise of a necessity for national security. By the way, your chance of being killed in a terrorist act, either domestic or abroad, is about 1 in 20 million. The likelihood of dying from a bee or wasp sting is 1 in 72,000 and the chance of dying in your car on the way to work is 1 in 303. Obviously, insects and the automotive industry are waging a much more successful Jihad against us than the Islamists could ever hope to wage. However, with carefully controlled propaganda from a well scripted press, we have been duped into surrendering nearly all of our civil liberties in the name of security from a terrorist act.

The quest for total government control shows no signs of stopping anytime soon. Just when it appears that they have finally gotten their hands in just about everything, they pull yet another rabbit out of the hat. They will stop at nothing to achieve the ultimate pinnacle of a surveillance state where every person may be logged into the system, tracked, surveilled, and controlled using every method conceivable that they have at their disposal. Just this week during the summer of 2013 former congressman Ron Paul wrote: "What collecting it all does mean is that our every electronic interaction is stored indefinitely by the federal government for possible future use against us should we ever fall out of government favor by, for example, joining a pro-peace organization, joining a pro-gun organization, posting statements critical of government spying on our Facebook pages or elsewhere. This massive database will be used, and perhaps has already been used, to keep us in line. The absence of meaningful congressional oversight- unless cheerleading counts as oversight- means that no one will put the brakes on people like Keith Alexander whose "passion" to "protect" us is taking us into totalitarianism." Not long after Ron Paul released this statement a bill came before the United States House of Representatives geared to reduce funding to the NSA and its surveillance programs. The bill was sponsored by Michigan Republican Justin Amash and co-sponsored by Michigan Democrat John Conyers and others. The Obama Administration raised a serious alarm regarding halting NSA surveillance and released this statement through White House spokesman Jay Carney: "We oppose the current effort in the House to hastily dismantle one of our Intelligence Community's counter terrorism tools." In a last minute attempt to ensure the bill wouldn't pass, the White House dispatched General Keith Alexander, Head of the NSA, to Capitol Hill to blackmail, (whoops did I say blackmail?) I meant urge law makers to vote down the amendment in separate, closed-door sessions with Republicans and Democrats. In the end, the amendment was defeated by the votes of 83 Democrats and 134 Republicans to continue the NSA spying program. With a small amount of investigation, it turns out that the 217 House members who voted against stopping the NSA dragnet receive twice as much campaign funding from the defense and intelligence industry as the 205 members who voted against NSA spying. Sold! Our 4th Amendment goes to the highest bidder. A complete list of those members who voted "NO' to the amendment to curtail NSA spying, can be found at www. techdirt.com. Perhaps these Representatives should not be re-elected since they place so little value on our right to privacy.

In another alarming development, President Obama signed Executive Order- HIV Care Continuum Initiative on July 13, 2013, and it was released without media fanfare on July 15th. The Executive Order would make HIV testing of persons between 15-65 years of age compulsory. According to the White House, it is an attempt to improve health outcomes for people living with HIV and is our answer to the ongoing HIV epidemic. Let's examine this epidemic. HIV infection rates peaked in the 1980's and has steadily decreased since then to the relatively stable 50,000 new cases per year for the last several years. HIV has dramatically decreased in women. 66% of new infections are in gay men with a growing number of those in gay black men although it is still more prevalent among gay white men. Transmission due to IV drug use is down and transmission from mother to baby is down. In contrast, 25.8 million people in the United States have diabetes and 1.9 million cases arise each year. The estimated cost of diabetes in 2007 due to direct health care cost and lost work wages were over 174 billion dollars. Incidentally, incidences in type II diabetes have also been linked to chronic exposure to electromagnetic pollution like Wi-Fi, radiofrequency, and cell phone signals. Nonetheless, the point I'm trying to make is that HIV is targeting a very specific group of individuals who are contracting it due to their chosen lifestyle. Diabetes is ravaging everyone. So why would President Obama sign an executive order recommending every man, woman, and child between 15-65 be tested for HIV? My gut feeling tells me that it is a covert way to sneak DNA data basing in on the segment of the population that did not get data based with a heel-stick at birth. I could be wrong, but I am probably not too far off base.

Unfortunately, the surveillance state is finally in place and apparently here to stay. Everything one does leaves a fingerprint behind that someone, somewhere can track. The mere action of wearing most clothing can actually have you tracked if it contains RFID tags. The most "transparent" State Department to ever grace the White House has exponentially worsened this fact. Steve Chapman, the columnist and writer with the Chicago Tribune, summed it up nicely: "George W. Bush and Dick Cheney spent eight years choking personal privacy to within an inch of its life. After they were done, Barack Obama showed up, expressed heartfelt sympathy and stood on its throat." For the past several years our government has essentially stood up and shot the finger at the fourth amendment of our Constitution. Hopefully, their excuse for monitoring millions of innocent people to find the handful of dangerous ones will soon fall on deaf ears as the public grows wise to their agenda.

CHAPTER 12
The Enemy Within

"For we hear certain ones are walking disorderly among you,
not working at all but meddling
with what does not concern them."
–2Thessalonians 3:11

The struggle for freedom is not easy in a world that has vilified the United States Constitution and portrayed freedom itself to be a relatively horrible state of being. Unfortunately, a large segment of the population has become complacent and found it easier to take refuge in mindless "barn animal" existence in which they can live check to check without ever displaying independent thought. This has not come to fruition coincidentally, but has been cultivated over several decades through social engineering; intentionally poor education and surreptitious control measures disguised as national security programs. Our freedoms were not taken overnight by an outside force akin to Nazi Germany rolling into Poland and enforcing martial law, but rather were taken a little bit at a time as most of us were convinced to freely surrender them. Big government and socialism has a very strong appeal to the lower socioeconomic classes that are relatively content eking out an existence as long as most of their needs are covered by the government. Some people, however, want more than the freedom to not work and seek an upwardly mobile existence rather than the economic slavery that so many people have been duped into accepting. Freedom is not pretty and is difficult to contain, thus government has been trying to stifle it, leaving us with only the illusion of freedom. True freedom gives me the right to offend you, and you the right to be offended, without either one of us petitioning for legislation from the government to limit the exchange. Freedom is like your one alcoholic uncle that only comes around at holidays, drinks himself into oblivion, teases your aunt for being a lesbian and tells you all kinds of secret stories about your parents and their younger years that are less than flattering. He gets everyone riled up and then leaves, only to be invited back again next year for the sheer entertainment value. Rather than allow our inebriated uncle his voice and tolerating his antics, we now seek Supreme Court regulations to limit his drinking, force him into treatment, and censor his speech or risk a civil lawsuit or hate-crime charge.

The federal government has long used political provocateurs in the civilian world to advance the "political correctness" agenda. More laws have been passed in the last two decades that supposedly protect certain societal minorities rather than the majority of the population than ever before in human history. These laws protect no one and serve only to forward the government's agenda of control. Political correctness laws have only served to fill the civil and criminal court dockets with problems and issues that should have been settled in a break room, not a courtroom. We will never legislate away the evils and taboos of society. What we have allowed to happen is government control of a large portion of society that can no longer operate in societal settings with true freedom of speech or actions. Nowhere is that more evident than in the workplace.

Regardless of the color of one's skin, if you perform horribly at your job, your employer should be able to terminate you without needing a team of attorneys to defend against a racism charge. The most blatant form of racism comes from the government itself in the form of affirmative action quotas. Many colleges and businesses that accept partial funding from the federal government are required to fulfill federal affirmative action quotas by hiring or accepting a certain percentage of minorities regardless of whether or not they are qualified. This is the pinnacle of racism. For the government to force institutions to lower their standards for some minorities, based on the government's acknowledgement that they are substandard, is a slap in the face to both the institution and the applicant. Unfortunately, the government has done such a good job at mainstreaming social engineering that we will probably never see it end, but rather continue to worsen. Political correctness and social engineering are forms of control intended to restrict freedom in the most surreptitious manner ever conceived. This might not seem readily evident to you, but give it some thought and you will come to realize that I am correct.

The most recent governmental attempt at social engineering comes hand in hand with the Obama brain-mapping program. In July 2013 the government announced that it's hiring a "Behavioral Insights Team" to help government and society operate more efficiently. I am all for the government working more efficiently, but I doubt a team of psychologists on the payroll will accomplish anything. Society, on the other hand, does not need influence from the government. The Behavioral Insight Team will be tasked with making use of the "Nudge Effect" to make Obama's socialist policies more palatable to the general public. Nudging involves providing subtle hints to the public through major media resources to direct their decision making on a certain topic to the advantage of the one nudging. The theory is based upon the book, Nudge, written by Cass Sunstein and Richard Thaler. You may remember from earlier in this book that Cass Sunstein was one of Obama's Czars and is a far left liberal and a known eugenicist. Moreover, White House documents are referring to the Behavioral Insights Team as the Nudge Squad and over a dozen government agencies will be working with this group or groups similar. Not surprisingly, one of the agencies involved with the Nudge Squad is the Department of Health and Human Services to help facilitate a better public acceptance of Obama Care. According to Michael Thomas, an economist at Utah State University, "nudging assumes a small group of people in government know better about choices than the individuals making them." Perhaps we should give the government a nudge by always refusing to pay our taxes for several years and nudging the government into operating on a budget like every other corporation and individual. We currently have a runaway government bent on controlling us in every manner and starving it financially will ultimately be our only recourse.

For those readers still of the belief that the government is surveilling and controlling only the fraction of the public that may be tied to terrorism, a very important document recently released may set you wise. One of the documents released by Edward Snowden to the Washington Post came to the public attention in August of 2013. According to an internal audit by the NSA itself, it has overstepped privacy laws and its legal authority thousands of times per year with regard to domestic surveillance. In one document NSA personnel were instructed to remove details and substitute more generic language in reports to the Justice Department and the Office of the Director of National Intelligence. In another document, it was brought to light that the Foreign Intelligence Surveillance Court was not informed of new collection methods until after they were in use for many months. The new methods were then ruled as unconstitutional by the FISA Court and a FISA court Judge commented that the "ability to police United States spying programs is limited." Contrary to statements made by NSA Director Keith Alexander to congress, we now know that the vast databases exist that include transcripts, facsimiles, telex, and voice and computer generated data such as call records and texts. These huge databases have code names like MARINA, PINWALE, XKEYSCORE and DISHFIRE for those that are interested.

The documents that Edward Snowden released regarding the NSA spying programs were not acquired by him during his employment with Booze Allen. Prior to being hired by Booze Allen, a private intelligence contractor, Snowden worked for DELL Computers based out of Austin, Texas. David Fink, spokesman for DELL, declined comment about Snowden's employment with DELL and commented that DELL's customer, the NSA, had asked them not to speak publicly about him. The only internet provider not named in the Snowden documents was Amazon Web Services. However, rumor had it that AWS had been in talks with the CIA to create a "secret" private cloud for them outside the United States for workloads that they would prefer to keep in-country. The rumor became fact when IBM contested the contract award to the General Accountability Office which ruled in their favor and recommended contract re-negotiations. So, if everyone is in bed with everyone within the computer and ISP world, do we really have any expectation of privacy while doing any work on a computer, especially if connected to the internet? My gut feeling is "no" since the NSA, CIA, and probably every other alphabet agency has negotiated deals with most if not all cell providers, computer manufacturers and internet providers.

The government has long fostered relationships with private industries where new ideas and technologies can be researched and developed cheaper and more efficiently than completely within the government bureaucracy. The private industries, in turn, can sell their product to the government at a significant profit. However, at the intelligence level, this government-industry relationship was taken several steps further than a strictly research and development relationship. Intelligence agencies sought out potentially useful upcoming technologies in the private sector and set about forming symbiotic partnerships with the companies in question. Most were more than happy to do their patriotic duty, for a price and signed on the intelligence based operations. Cell phone providers provided office space, access to records, access to fiber optic cables, and splitters to listen in on those fiber optic cables to the NSA. Until very recently, most cell phone companies denied having solidified this relationship with the NSA until the cat was out of the bag. Like teenagers at their first prom, cell providers claimed they were only giving the NSA a little hug for the money and there were no privacy concerns to worry about. However, several months later they were starting to show and there was no denying that the unsuspecting public had gotten a little more than a hug on prom night!

The cooperation between intelligence agencies and the private sector has gotten much more complex than merely contractual obligations for a desired product or service. Insidiously, spycraft has been taken out of the sole proprietorship of the NSA, CIA and DIA and contracted out to the "pseudo-civilian" contractors. Private sector intelligence gathering has become an extremely lucrative business with a multitude of privately held companies battling for government contracts. The possession of a government clearance is now openly traded on the free market with many companies actively seeking former government employees with varying levels of security clearance. Government intelligence agencies have become revolving doors for personnel to supply the growing market for independent contractors with security clearances. Author Tim Shorrock, in his book Spies for Hire: The Secret World of Intelligence Outsourcing, does a great job of exposing this dirty little secret that has actually worsened since it was published in 2008. As of 2008, apparently 70% of the country's intelligence work was being contracted out to private intelligence companies. In 2006, more than half of the employees at the National Counter Terrorism Center were private sector contract employees and the NCTC's control room itself was designed by private sector engineers from Walt Disney Imagineering. Contractors now make up more than half of the workforce of the National Clandestine Service and private businesses doing business with the NSA has grown from 144 companies in 2001 to over 5,400 now. Most of the text messages, cell phone, and e-mail intercepts provided by the NSA are actually the work of companies like SAIC, CACI International and Northrop Grumman which are responsible for the interception and analysis of the data.

The CIA has not been exempt from making excessive use of private contractors as have other agencies. It is estimated that 60 percent of its annual budget is spent on private contractors. Private contractors now outnumber the fulltime workforce of the CIA and are often allowed to perform the same tasks as lifelong agents. Within the CIA, contractors wear a colored badge to differentiate them from the actual government hired agents and are known as "green-badges." According to retired CIA field officer Robert Baer, "many of the green-badges are former CIA employees, often returning to the same jobs they had before they retired and earning double or triple the salaries they made as government employees." As of 2013, the number of top secret clearances held by government employees was 791,200 while civilian contractors held approximately 598,763 top secret clearances. Aside from the obvious ethical issues regarding this, many top-secret clearance, non-governmental employees, the sheer cost to the taxpayers has become astounding. The majority of the intelligence community budget is being devoted to finding private sector intelligence contractors at the taxpayers' expense. This privatization of the intelligence community though "private-public partnerships" has had a deleterious effect on both our intelligence community and our right to privacy as citizens. It is difficult enough to escape true government intrusion into one's privacy, however with governmental tentacles in a myriad of private companies performing data gathering, privacy becomes only a pipe dream.

In 2007 an interoperability demonstration was put on at the GEOINT 2007 Symposium in San Antonio, Texas. Sponsored by the United States Geospatial Intelligence Foundation, the demonstration gave us a very good example of the key players involved in domestic surveillance. In this demonstration, an alleged Cuban vessel carrying spent nuclear fuel was to be tracked and analyzed as it headed for United States shores. The mock situation involved the big three players, Booze Allen, Northrop Grumman, and L3 Communications as well as lesser known companies like ESRI, SRA International, PCI, Geomatics, MetaCarta, and Lockheed Martin. ESRI provides mapping software to the NGA, SRA International supplies intelligence, surveillance and reconnaissance software to the NSA, PCI is a Canadian company that sells software for quickly processing and interpreting geospatial imagery and MetaCarta makes software for counterterrorism use in analyzing lines of text for geographic references. Remember, this is all from 2007, so imagine the advances that have been made since then. It is evident that the tools used for geospatial intelligence that allow agencies to share information among themselves and with law enforcement are now the sole proprietorship of private companies. One has to question the oversight that exists when such powerful tools are placed into the hands of civilian contractors, many of whom have top-secret clearances. It's bad enough that the potential for abuse of such technology is present under usual government oversight; however, with private contractors at the helm there appears to be little to no oversight regarding its use domestically. Of course, this may be happening intentionally to give the government plausible deniability when the complaints start surfacing of domestic spying, as they have over the last decade.

The government's reason for outsourcing so much of the intelligence budget is that 90% of the nation's commerce energy and transportation companies are privately held and therefore most play a role in homeland security. Private intelligence contractors were more than happy to join in at a heavy cost to the taxpayers. Booze Allen Hamilton and Bearing Point were awarded extremely lucrative contracts to provide intelligence services to the DHS as a new form of capitalism was created that serves the needs of government. As Tim Shorrock wrote, "Once private and public interests are merged, then the need for oversight disappears, along with regulation and other institutions designed as a brake….or as watchdogs against corruption." We have more than reached the point of no return as far as outsourcing of foreign and domestic and intelligence gathering. Most of the experts on the topic of intelligence outsourcing have historically blamed the Bush Administration for letting it get so out of control. Most thought that the President and Administration to follow Bush would begin to reign in the 70% plus of the intelligence budget spent on private contractors. They were wrong. Under the Obama

Administration, approximately 1,931 private companies work on programs related to counter terrorism, homeland security, and intelligence in more than 10,000 locations across the country. In August 2013, President Obama appointed a high level group of outside experts, as promised, to assess the government's use of intelligence and communication technologies. The "outside" experts included Michael Morell, recently acting head of the CIA, and former National Security Council staff member, Richard Clarke. The other two members included Cass Sunstein, former information and regulatory Czar under President Obama who championed federal agents infiltrating conspiracy theory online social networks to raise doubts about any factual premises. Peter Swire is the other non-intelligence member who was also an Obama Administration official. According to the Guardian, "the review of the United States surveillance programs which Barack Obama promised would be conducted by an independent and outside panel of experts looks set to consist of four Washington insiders with close ties to the security establishment." Of course, by using the term "outside" he may have meant that brief amount of time the members spent exposed to the elements from the cab to the door of the White House. Essentially President Obama has appointed a group of foxes to determine if the hen house has adequate protections from intrusion by foxes. Sadly he will spin this issue into a highly fabricated heap of dung that the major media will repeatedly play to the public until they swallow it and see it his way. Nudge! Nudge!

Amazingly, just as Obama is operating a kangaroo court to determine if government spying on the public has gone astray, the NSA offers up one of its own to a truth starved public. Hoping if they admitted to a handful of minor infractions that the public outcry for truth would end, the NSA announced what was supposed to be a bombshell of information to the media.

The announcement was made by the NSA and President Obama that thousands of non-terrorism related emails of innocent Americans were "accidentally" collected by the NSA. This was yet another lie from the least transparent administration to ever set foot in the White House. The NSA has a multi-billion dollar budget and unrivaled technological sophistication which allows them carte blanche access to every form of communication. They know what they are collecting! However, the more important announcement by the NSA was that one of its analysts deliberately abused its surveillance systems. Anonymous NSA officials admitted that some NSA employees and contractors had abused their positions to monitor love interests, girlfriends, spouses, and ex-spouses. According to the officials, "the problem is infrequent but common enough to garner its own spycraft label as LOVEINT." Leaping to the rescue of the NSA, Senate Intelligence Committee Chairwoman Diane Feinstein, lifelong liberal democrat and professional liar, stated that the number of NSA personnel involved in violating procedures was "roughly one per year." She has promised to review each one of those cases in detail and report back to the American public with an excuse that will certainly be fanciful and entertaining. However, the recent admission of abuse of power to monitor love interests may be the crux to the entire problem of nonconsensual experimentation with electromagnetic weapons.

As you've read, a good majority of the surveillance work has been outsourced to private contractors who have unclear oversight if any oversight at all. Edward Snowden was actually working as a contractor with Booze Allen Hamilton when he came forward with his documents that were made accessible to him through his security clearance. While Snowden seems to have taken the much more difficultly traveled moral high ground, most contractors obviously are not. The admission by the NSA about employees and contractors alike targeting romantic interest through LOVEINT brings up some very serious questions. Many of the victims of nonconsensual experimentation with electromagnetic weapons are female and a great percentage of them are complaining of sexual assault along with their targeting. Could it be that the proper pseudonym should be RAPEINT for what is happening rather than LOVEINT? Unfortunately, the admission by the NSA about counter surveillance somewhat sugarcoated the issue. The truth is that the system being used for monitoring is also a weapons system capable of manipulating the targeted person, not just visualizing them. This came to light years ago in 1991 by yet another NSA insider, John St. Clair Akewei in a court case filed against the NSA. In John St. Clair Akewei vs NSA, Ft Meade, MD (Civil Action 92-0449), Akewei outlined the technologies being used to surveil, control, and manipulate certain individuals. His comment in the suit was "the NSA/DoD has developed proprietary advanced digital equipment which can remotely analyze all objects whether man-made or organic that has electrical activity." "With this technology NSA personnel can unobtrusively tap into any communication device in existence. This included computers, telephones, radio and video based devices, printers, car electronics, and even the minute electrical fields in humans." He went on to explain the frequencies needed to target certain areas of the human body and the effects that targeting will have. Around that same time frame, Pravda News in Russia published an article by John Fleming entitled "The Shocking Menace of Satellite Surveillance" in which he outlined much of the same technological capabilities and warned of its potential use on an unsuspecting public. I personally spoke to Mr. Akewei before writing my first book on this topic, A New Breed. His history, credentials, and lawsuit appear to be legitimate to me. Of course, in the 1990's both

Fleming and Akewei's comments were mostly seen as science fiction and rejected by the press other than conspiracy theory sites. However, in lieu of what is coming out now about an unbridled NSA, using mostly private contractors, perhaps they were both merely way ahead of their time.

Hopefully more of these enemies within will seek the moral high ground as did Akewei, Fleming, Tice, and Snowden. It is certainly the more difficult road to travel as I am certain these four men would attest to. However, it's time we the people begin to demand ethical behavior from our government which includes leaving our right to privacy intact and ceasing their nonconsensual experimentation on an unsuspecting public. The fact is that the technology has come so far that the systems that are being used for surveillance are also weapon systems used for control. It may have been unbelievable in prior decades, but the science research and the complaints of its widespread use are in the open now and cannot to being ignored. We owe it to future generations to get it under control now or our children and grandchildren will see their humanity reduced to nothing more than them being another worker bee in a hive of total governmental control.

CHAPTER 13

Valley of Elah

"And David put his hand on his bag and took out a stone and slung it and struck the Philistine on his forehead."

—1 Samuel 17:49

David was the youngest of four sons to Jesse, an Ephrathite from Bethlehem. His three older brothers had followed Saul to the war against the Philistines and were camped in the Valley of Elah. David, just a boy, would take time from tending his father's sheep to bring food and drink to his brothers in Elah. Goliath, a Philistine of considerable stature, over 9 feet tall, would come out at the same time each day to ridicule the army of Israel and challenge whichever champion they chose to fight him. This had gone on repeatedly for forty days. The custom at the time was for each army to send one of their champions onto the field of battle in representation of the entire army rather than each entire army go into battle. David happened to be visiting at the time Goliath was issuing his daily decree for an Israeli champion to face him in battle. Seeing that the soldiers trembled in fear at the sight of Goliath, David took five smooth stones from a stream, his staff and a sling onto the battlefield to fight Goliath. Goliath was shocked that they would allow a boy with a stick to face him in his armor and accoutrements of battle.

David said to Goliath, "you come against me with your sword and spear but I come against you in the name of the living God." He reached into his bag taking out a stone; he slung it striking Goliath in the forehead. Goliath fell facedown and David took the Philistine's sword and cut off his head with it, thus winning the battle for Israel.

The story of David and Goliath has as much significance today as it did at the time it actually occurred. An entire army of men, none of which felt competent to defeat Goliath, had failed to win the battle against the Philistines and their giant champion. However, a young boy, correctly armed with the belief in God was able to defeat their giant with a sling and a stone. We find ourselves today in the same predicament as Saul's army facing an ever growing government looming over us like a giant that cannot be defeated. Perhaps the American public, like Saul's army, has continually used the wrong weapons to facilitate a defeat of the giant. The reason that each army at that time sent out their single champion to do battle was that it was thought that the battle was actually spiritual in nature. The gods, or god, and one champion would triumph over the gods or god of the other in spiritual warfare, using the flesh and blood of each man to facilitate the physical battle. With regard to nonconsensual experimentation with electromagnetic weapons, we are indeed the unwilling participants in spiritual warfare. The traditional armor of weapons will not defeat this technology; it must be something more powerful and more ethereal than what would traditionally be used for other lesser battles.

When I first began to write about this topic and conducted thousands of email, phone and live interviews with victims of this technology, I immediately noticed a sense of defeat in most of them. The number of victims emailing me has grown exponentially since 2006, yet I still sense a feeling of defeat and isolation from most of them. Despite more information about electronic harassment online than ever before, most victims feel like they are alone in the fight against it. That is a normal feeling to have but is far from the truth.

In my first book, A New Breed, I chronicled the torture that was endured by Mallory at the hands of a former FBI agent who has been given access to advanced surveillance technology to use for his own gain. Being a Christian, I was able to turn to a number of clergy members and Christian friends and confide in them about the torment we were going through. Law enforcement agencies humored us, lawyers ignored us and doctors usually wanted to diagnose us as mentally ill for what we knew we were up against. However, the pastors and Christian friends that were approached believed us implicitly and offered a different perspective on the topic. The concept of spiritual warfare has been taught in Christian circles for many, many years. The celestial battle between good and evil has been raging on since the dawn of man. Don't worry, when several pastors I spoke with about our torment told me that we were chest deep in spiritual warfare I balked, just as you are currently doing as you try and make sense of this chapter. "We are not fighting demons, but men stalking us, breaking into our homes and using electromagnetic weapons on us." Several trusted pastors that I confided in finally made me understand that while as victims and perpetrators, we were the flesh and blood in a much larger celestial war between the forces of dark and light. The war between good and evil was here before man was ever created, patiently waiting for us to take part in the battles. Unfortunately, evil has some new technology in the game that could be equally used for good as I have described earlier in the book.

As I set out on my journey to learn more about the spiritual warfare component of this battle, I realized very quickly that we were never alone in this fight. A number of Christian pastors had been writing and speaking about electronic harassment, nonconsensual experimentation with microchipping and directed energy technology, and relating it to spiritual warfare. Specifically, they have been relating it to the Book of Revelation in the Bible and it all seems to ring pretty true. The Book of Revelation, written by John the Elder, usually accepted to be the Apostle John of the Gospels, was written on the rocky island of Patmos in the Aegean Seas off the coast of modern day Turkey. It was used as a Roman penal settlement during Domitian's reign and many believe the Book of Revelation to be the result of the many persecutions of Christians carried out by Domitian. Domitian reigned at a time when the Romans were enforcing emperor worship and those that held the belief that "Jesus is Lord" found persecution and martyrdom at the hands of the Roman government. The Apostle John had been exiled to the island of Patmos for his atrocities as a Christian missionary. This scenario does not sound much different from the adversities that the Christians and non-Christians alike are facing today with regard to a government that seeks to control every aspect of humanity.

Pastor Perry Stone has long preached about the dangers of RFID and microchipping as it pertains to the Book of Revelation. In one of his sermons he went in depth into the various types of microchips currently used today and some still under research for use in the future. Of course, as a Christian Pastor, he relates this to be the mark of the beast as it is described in Revelation. If one goes to YouTube and searches for "Perry Stone on End Times and RFID" you can see a video of this sermon and others similar to it. Not surprisingly, he suffered a tremendous backlash against his stand on micro-chipping from Christians, non-Christians, liberals and conservatives' in a myriad of online blog sites. One thing I have learned from writing and speaking on this topic is that once you pull the pin on the truth grenade and get a direct hit, people are gunning for you from every direction. The fact that this happened to Perry Stone makes me believe him even more than I already did from my own research.

Grant R. Jeffrey is another minister who has also written on the topic of electronic harassment and the growing surveillance state. His book entitled, "Shadow Government-How the Secret Global Elite is Using Surveillance Against You," was released in 2010 and sold mostly in Christian book stores. It was written prior to 2010, but details at length the upcoming surveillance technologies that would be used by the NSA to invade our privacy. He mentioned cell phone interception, email surveillance, DNA profiling, and biometric surveillance as the same technology that the NSA has admitted using in 2013 to spy on the public. Moreover, in Chapter 6 of this book, he goes into detail about new weapons in the arsenal of the new world order. These include directed energy weapons comprised of non-lethal pulsed, electromagnetic, and radio-frequency based technologies. He also mentions the first use of a particle beam weapon in Baghdad in 2004. An Iraqi soldier, Majid Al-Ghazali, described a tank based weapon that fired lightning bolts at a bus filled with insurgents. The bus was reduced to the size of a Volkswagen Beetle and the bodies of insurgents were rendered to less than 18 inches in length. Within hours after the attack, American military bulldozers and work crews buried the vehicles and misshapen bodies to prevent further observation. Interestingly, he also mentions the "voice of God" weapon, which has already been created, to project a verbal or visual message into the mind of an enemy combatant. This is exactly the technology that thousands of people in the United States are complaining of being victimized by in 2013. He finishes the chapter mentioning weather warfare using HAARP as well as nano-technological weapons, genetic weapons, and thermobaric weapons. All of the advances in weapon technology that he wrote about prior to 2009 have come to pass. Each chapter of his book is well referenced with legitimate sources from which he derived his information.

The reason I've included this chapter is to point out a few things that should be obvious to you by now, if they weren't already. We, as humanity, are David in the modern version of the story of David and Goliath. We have allowed government to grow so large that the traditional weapons of battle will no longer be effective in subduing it. Political correctness, apathy, and a sense of helplessness have muddied our moral and ethical judgment when it comes to electing and re-electing our leaders. Secondly, Christian pastors have been writing, preaching and warning about this technology and the day that it would come for some time. Most victims of the technology have written their doctors, law enforcement officials and legislators about their plight only to find disbelief and the recommendation that they seek help from a mental health professional. In my conversations with victims, I've sensed that many see Christianity and religion as just another form of control. However, there is a distinction between the true Church and religion that may not be clearly understood by most of the people that express that feeling. The Church is the sum total of all the people who believe in Christ and his teaching; it has absolutely nothing to do with any religion and its rules or sanctions. The fact is the Christians have seen this fight coming for a long time. In fact, John saw it coming when he wrote Revelation while imprisoned on Patmos around AD 80-90. Christians may refer to the phenomenon as spiritual warfare rather than electronic harassment but we are both referring to the same issue and its effects on humanity. Perhaps individuals targeted by this horrific technology should be reaching out to their Christian friends and clergy to assist in the fight rather than assume that religion is part of the problem.

I am certain that I will receive a number of emails for starting each chapter of this book with a Biblical verse and including this chapter. Hopefully, I have clearly stated the reason for its inclusion within the chapter. It's quite possible that ancient scripts from other religions may also touch on the same topic as Revelation in the Christian Bible. However, being a Christian, I can only write about what I believe to be true and have knowledge of based upon my own reading and teachings. I am a Christian but I would like to be clear that I am not including this chapter to be evangelistic in any way. I am merely stating what I found to be true in my conversations with Christian friends and my understanding of literature on this topic from Christian writers. Everyone is certainly entitled to whatever system of belief or non-belief they choose to partake in. However, it has been my experience that most of my Christian friends understand what electronic harassment is and relate it very well to the teachings of both Revelation and spiritual warfare in the Bible.

CHAPTER 14
The Hidden Agenda

"All the ways of man are pure in his own eyes,
but the Lord weighs the spirit."
–Proverbs 16:2

Many people reading the book may be finding it to be their first introduction to the topic of electromagnetic technology intended to control the minds and bodies of the targeted. While the number of victims has grown exponentially over the last decade, I assure you this is not a novel topic. The research into electromagnetic control technologies has been so covert and insidious that it has only been recently that we can piece the puzzle together. In earlier chapters I touched upon the surface of directed energy technology, nonconsensual experimentation and early issues of control technology. It should be clear to the reader that this technology has been leading one direction to the eventual control of the masses. As I have stated before, guns and taxes cannot control everyone but globally applied electromagnetic technology certainly has the ability. For instance, in 1974 when MKULTRA researcher Dr. Jose Delgado testified to congress he stated, "Man does not have the right to develop his own mind...we must electronically control the brain." However, by the 1980's, practicing at the Ramon y Cajal

Hospital in Madrid, Spain, Delgado's comments had changed from implantation to broadcasting. In an interview, Delgado related that electromagnetic broadcasting had been, "developed to a state of effectiveness and could be utilized at up to three kilometers." One can see how the technology had advanced from the "stimoreceiver" and brain implants to electromagnetic broadcasting from 1969 to 1980.

Indeed, several of the earliest complaints of broadcasted mind control technology date back to 1988 when several prisoners from the Utah State Prison system voiced some very unusual complaints. David Fratus, Robert LaSalle, Frank Moxley, and Robert Varner were all prisoners at Utah State Prison. All penned affidavits describing electromagnetic torture while imprisoned that included hearing the voices of tormentors in their heads that responded to their thoughts with punishment. All of the prisoners reported having ringing in their ears from which they could sometimes distinguish voices and that the voices responded to their thoughts. Another Utah State prisoner, James Gardner, in a 1991 affidavit commented that "the mental voice communication process I am describing definitely involved thought comprehension because the voices were able to respond to what I was thinking." All of the former prisoners also described headaches, debilitation and incapacitation as if "a giant magnet was pulling me to the floor." Around that same time in 1987 a truck driver Martin Mack, described a similar experience of electronic harassment during which he suffered painful stings, thermal heating, and what he described as voices in his head that responded back to his thoughts. In his own words he stated, "Somehow, they were able to make me hear and also pick up on the process of my hearing-hear what I heard, as if my head was an antenna." Obviously, the early control research that began with MKULTRA as "hands on" research using drugs and electro-convulsive therapy advanced as technology allowed it to be done remotely.

MKULTRA was a group of subprojects that included the use of micro-chipping, drugs, electric shock, and other modalities to induce mind control. However, as I described in the chapter on MKULTRA, these subprojects also included studies into group behavior, individual behavior, and child behavior. It has been of the utmost importance to the CIA to not only control the individual but also population groups. As electromagnetic technology advanced, it too was studied as to its effects on groups of individuals as well. It has been alleged that the People's Temple mass suicide in Guyana at the direction of its founder Jim Jones, may have included mind control technology. Several financial supporters of the People's Temple had loose CIA ties as well as ties to the Symbionese Liberation Army that brainwashed Patty Hearst. As a matter of fact, after Hearst was arrested by the Los Angeles Police Department, the doctors that were called in to evaluate her were Dr. Martin Orne, Robert Lifton, and Dr. Jolyon West. Orne and West were known MKULTRA subcontractors and Lifton was the founder of the CIA contracted Human Ecology Fund, a known front company for MKULTRA research.

Another mass suicide in March 1997 when members of the UFO Cult, Heaven's Gate, all committed suicide by drinking a similar potion to the one given by the People's Temple victims. The mass suicide occurred in the Rancho Santa Fe, a suburb of San Diego, as the Hale-Bopp Comet approached the earth. The website for Heaven's Gate was hosted by the web server Spacestar which was also used by SAIC (Scientific Applications International Corps), a CIA sub-contractor. Another interesting connection to the Heaven's Gate Cult is the murder of business man and CIA operative Ian Stuart Spiro. Spiro's family, who lived near the cult in Rancho Santa Fe, was found shot to death in November of 1992 while Spiro was found dead from cyanide poisoning in his SUV later at the western edge of the Anza-Borrego Desert. Spiro was allegedly a Heaven's Gate member and despite attempts by law enforcement to portray the events as a murder-suicide scenario, his brother-in -law contends it was CIA or Mossad related.

Based upon known existing documents released by FOIA regarding MKULTRA and other mind control research projects, it is obvious they were attempting to learn how to control individuals. The next logical step would be to figure out how to exert the same control mechanisms in groups of individuals. It has been alleged that many of the cults, like the ones previously mentioned, were actually created by government agencies as testing units for group control technologies. When one traces the origins of many of the known cults there indeed usually turns up some individuals with known CIA ties of one form or another. This would also explain the known testing on prisoners, children in orphanages and hospitalized mentally ill patients that we know occurred through released records. The groups previously mentioned are easy targets for nonconsensual experimentation as they lack the usual human rights safeguards in place for those not in some type of detention. Sadly, many individuals from those institutions have voiced complaints of experimentation but their history discredits them in many people's eyes. Moreover, we've seen what I term "social outliers" used as guinea pigs for electromagnetic weapons research most recently. People with minor mental health issues, prior or current drug problems, and minor criminal histories are often the victims of the current electromagnetic experimentation we are seeing now. As I have stated earlier in the book, their personal history is enough to self-discredit them as far as getting legitimate complaints heard and acted upon by appropriate agencies.

Fast forward to today, we have over 300,000 people in the United States voicing complaints of electronic harassment which includes directed energy attacks and synthetic telepathic harassment. It sounds unbelievable at first until you delve deeper into the complaints and the history of the technology. For the past decade it has largely been written off as mental illness by the medical community and the subject of taunts by the major media. Often as victims of this type of technology would come forward they would be minimized by the press as "tin foil hat" people. This occurred due to the early efforts of victims to try and shield their brains from intrusion with aluminum covers of one type or another. Essentially it was an attempt at one protecting themselves from a form of technology they poorly understood with whatever means they could afford. Of course that form of shielding does not work and places the victim right into the scenario that the experiment intends, which is to stimulate mental illness in the victim. However, now with hundreds of thousands of people voicing complaints, numerous websites addressing the issue, numerous blogs popping up among victims and occasional accounts turning up in the major media, the medical community is going to have to step up and take notice. I would wager that within the next decade nearly every family in America will have at least one member voicing complaints of electronic harassment. Knowing how this research started and how it progressed as technology progressed should alarm the medical community that nonconsensual experimentation is occurring rather than an exponential rise in mental illness. We have known for some time that several technologies exist that are capable of putting voices in one's head to harass or subliminally control them. Therefore, when these complaints are voiced it can no longer be seen as a turnkey diagnosis of mental illness. Directed energy weapons are a fact of modern day society backed up by legitimate research while psychiatric diagnosis is still based solely on the whim and conjecture of the examiner with no basis in hard science.

The "tin foil hat" people got a small reprieve as leaks came forward in the press about the capabilities of the NSA. For years victims of electronic harassment have been complaining of cell phone spoofing, email tampering and text message spying in addition to their other complaints. As documents began to surface that detailed the extent of the NSA's electronic overreach, their complaints no longer seemed to be in the realm of science fiction. As this book is being written, the daily leaks about the extent of NSA spying on domestic citizens is so overwhelming that this book will be obsolete before it is released. Several years ago the NSA was allegedly only listening in on domestic calls made to foreigners in areas known to harbor terrorists as part of the Patriot Act. That lie surfaced as it was revealed that everyone's phone calls, texts, and emails are actually being subjected to surveillance whether you have terrorist affiliations or not. Of course, none of this would have surfaced in the major media had not several of their reporters and news agencies been victims as well.

The hidden agenda is actually not so hidden anymore. It's about as obvious as a giant pink elephant doing the meringue at a super bowl halftime show without a wardrobe failure to try and prolong its lackluster career a little while longer. Unfortunately, the United States has become the land of the controlled and the home of the apathetic. The wealthy class has long been controlled by taxation, the poor enslaved with welfare, and most recently, all of us controlled by surveillance. Our current administration has the same agenda as the United Nations and intends to be the enforcement branch of a One World Government, hence the strong push for gun control in this country, which coincidently is linked to electronic harassment very intimately. It does not surprise me, or any of the victims of electronic harassment, that every one of the recent mass shootings has been by an individual "hearing voices." Of course, the major media regurgitates the government's official line of turnkey diagnosing each shooter as paranoid schizophrenic that has played too many violent video games. Interestingly, they aren't attempting to censor video games at all. Guns, however, that is a different story entirely! The liberal left socialist agenda that is vehemently pushing for gun control stems from the dictates of every former communist, fascist, and socialist agenda. According to Joseph Stalin, "if the political opposition disarms, well and good. If it refuses to disarm, we shall disarm it ourselves."

Both the Aurora, Colorado shooting and the Sandy Hook shooting came to fruition surprisingly close to the time when the government was pushing for gun control, specifically of AR15 assault weapons. I am not trying to add to the proliferation of conspiracy theories abounding about these shootings but knowing something about control technology does make them suspect. The Sandy Hook shooter took his own life but what has been released about him through the media has been limited. Forensic toxicology showed no illicit drugs or pharmaceutical drugs in his system at autopsy so the reason we were given was too many violent video games and mental illness. The Aurora shooter was arrested in a limp state resting near his car in the theater parking lot and offered no resistance to arrest. According to one of the arresting officers, he did not appear to be under the influence of anything. However, the toxicology report has not been released and very little information about him has been released other than his conversion to Islam in prison. Is it possible that those two shooters were controlled to do what they did as part of a larger agenda regarding gun control? If reading some of the earlier chapters in this book does not have you at least contemplating the possibility, perhaps the next paragraph will!

The latest mass shooting was perpetuated by Aaron Alexis at the Washington Navy Yard. He killed 12 people with a shotgun and a handgun. Of course, initial stories in the major media reported him using an AR15, the gun of choice that many would like to see banned. Alexis was a Navy contractor with a security clearance and experience in the IT field. He had reported to the police that he thought he was being stalked and attacked with a microwave type device that was disrupting his sleep prior to the shooting. He also reported hearing the voices of his perpetrators in his head. Alexis cleared a background check in 2007 and was found eligible to handle "secret material" in 2008. One must wonder if his clearance allowed him information about directed energy weapons of which he was complaining about. Former friends of Mr. Alexis described him as polite and courteous and were shocked at his role in the murders. He did have two minor criminal offenses in his background and an alleged sleep disorder of insomnia which may have actually been sleep deprivation. Incidentally, all of the victims of electronic harassment I have interviewed report worsening of their attacks at night in order to sleep deprive them. I think it is likely that Aaron Alexis was a victim of electronic harassment and struck out to attack what he perceived as the source of his torture. Certainly, the etching on his shotgun, "this is my ELF weapon," points in that direction. Not unexpectedly, the shooting has led to yet another media outcry for gun control rather than a congressional hearing to expose the existence of psycho-tronic weapons. The governments hidden agenda is complete control, its weapons are vast and at the forefront its remarkable power of diversion. Rahm Emanuel, a crony of Barack Obama, said it best, "never let a serious crisis go to waste." Moreover, if a crisis doesn't exist, create one. As people begin waking up to the extreme overreach of the NSA and the IRS, Syria suddenly crossed Obama's "red line" and used biological weapons on its civilian population. The speculation as to whether we would strike Syria or not permeated the press and the public, taking the heat off of the NSA, IRS and hearings on Obama Care. Despite giving Syria a "red line" on camera, Obama denied saying it after our allies, congress, and the public disagreed with intervening in Syria's civil war. Insult was added to injury when Russian President Vladimir Putin saved the day by negotiating a surrender of chemical weapons with Syria, making Obama look foolish on the world stage. Another crisis was needed so we were given the Washington Navy Yard shooting to rekindle the gun control debates, which the government controlled media happily did. The shooting was not even over before claims were made on CBS, NBC and CNN that an AR-15 was used and socialists began their anti-gun rhetoric. Once again the NSA, IRS, Obama Care, Benghazi, and our border problems were able to be shuffled to the back burner and out of sight of the majority of the poorly informed public.

The most recent example of government control should awaken everyone to the hidden agenda. As I have stated before, the government operates through diversion and political theater. In October 2013, the government was shut down financially for a bit due to the non-passage of a continued government funding bill. In an attempt to defund Obama Care before its implication nationwide, Republicans attached a rider to the government funding bill that would exclude Obama Care. This came after Obama amended the original law almost nineteen times allowing some corporations, unions and Congress itself to opt out of the financially suicidal Obama Care. Obama Care is actually called The Patient Protection and Affordable Care Act but is anything but affordable and protects no one. Some of the issues with the act include the fact that it was passed without any of our legislators actually reading it. It fines corporations that hire greater than 50 full-time employees who are not offered insurance through their company. This has caused many companies to cut their employee roles down to mostly part-time status which is detrimental to those employees who depend on a full-time paycheck. A fine is also planned for individuals who choose not to purchase private insurance or participate in the federal insurance plan. However, the most troubling fact about Obama Care is that it will be administered by the IRS. Do you really want the IRS determining what healthcare you qualify for? As a physician, I believe Obama Care will do nothing but put a proof of insurance card in people's wallets but actually cover very little a patient may need when they find themselves affected by illness. Obama Care is mostly a covert form of taxation and has little to do with providing health care to the American public.

Nonetheless, the shutdown of the government itself due to the Obama Care debacle is where the hidden agenda could be found peeking its head out from under the corner of darkness. As the government shut down began on October 1, 2013 we saw historic memorials, national parks and some social programs like WIC and others temporarily close their services. Many non-essential federal employees also furloughed temporarily. However, the parts of the government that did not shut down should tell us something about our government. While many government employees went unpaid during the shutdown, the members of Congress and the President continued to draw their salaries. The shutdown also did not seem to delay the grand opening of the new NSA data collecting center in Utah which went online just prior to the shutdown. As a matter of fact, the shutdown had no effect on any of the various intelligence agencies or the Federal Bureau of Investigation. It should be very obvious that the lack of funding does not stop the watchers from watching!

CHAPTER 15
Pergola of Perdition

"Beware lest any man spoil you through philosophy
and vain deceit…"

–Colossians 2:8

"Ask not what your country can do for you, ask what you can do for your country," were the words of President John F. Kennedy in his inaugural address on January 20, 1961. Amazingly, a Democratic President preaching the value of individual responsibility would hardly be tolerated by the Democratic Party today. However, even as those words rolled off of President Kennedy's tongue, the welfare state had already rooted itself in the United States a quarter of a century earlier. During the Great Depression one quarter of the work force was unemployed at the same time severe drought had devastated the Midwest farmlands. People were suffering. President Franklin D. Roosevelt enacted a number of federal plans to get people back to work and bolster the economy. As fate would have it, World War II began and provided a greater impetus for economic recovery than any federal plan could have succeeded in doing. However, as the economy grew and the war came to an end, the federal welfare plans continued and were grown exponentially by each president that followed Roosevelt.

As the welfare state grew, so did the number of federal agencies created to handle the growing demand. This resulted in not only a growing number of citizens on the welfare programs, but an equally large number of people being employed by the federal government. As a matter of fact, on September 30, 2013, President Obama made the comment that, "the federal government is America's largest employer," in a speech regarding the certain horrors we face with a government shutdown. The comment was made glowingly but the fact that the federal government is our largest employer is more of a problem than a solution.

Currently, approximately 8% of the United States population or 29,900,000 people derive some or all of their financial support from government welfare programs. If one combines the prior statistics with the number of people employed by the government, the results are significant. Federal, State, and local governments employ 22.2 million workers nationwide, equaling 16.7% of the United States workforce with government employment rates rising in 37 states. President Obama was truthful, for once, in his comment that the federal government is our largest employer. The combined number of people directly deriving their existence from the government is approximately 52 million and growing each day. In nine states, the government employs one-fifth of all workers in the state. This is a serious issue when it comes time to try and enact change in governmental policies that may be found to be detrimental to the Constitution or the public as a whole.

The point is that the public in the United States has not been forced into servitude to the government in work or welfare. We have not been dragged across the Bridge of Sighs or forced at bayonet point down the Bataan Trail into indentured servitude. But rather, we have been bullied down the shaded path of least resistance that appeals to human nature's more apathetic side, with treats of reinforcement carefully laid out along the way to keep us racing in this desired direction. This uniquely American method of progress toward a socialistic society is something Karl Marx could have only dreamed about. Historically, the advance of a Socialist agenda typically meant killing or starving a large portion of society to force the rest into subservience. In America, the Socialists have achieved the same goals much more subtly and surreptitiously. President Clinton tried to slightly combat the shift toward government dependence in 1996 when he signed the Personal Responsibility and Work Opportunity Act to try and get more welfare recipients in the workforce. The act did reduce poverty and introduced many welfare recipients to the joy of personal responsibility by forcing them to seek employment. However, President Obama gutted the work requirements written into the Act disregarding the requirement that welfare recipients find work. Hopefully you can begin to see where this is going.

If one also factors in the number of people receiving Social Security backed disability income, the number of people living on the government dole is even larger. According to Bureau of Labor Statistics about 1.2 million Americans were on disability in 1968 with 51 full-time workers for each worker on disability. In 2013 a record 8.9 million workers collected disability with only 13 full-time workers for each worker on disability. The combined number of people in the United States getting a paycheck from the government is approximately 61 million people out of the 116 million full-time workers. The problem with these numbers is that individuals deriving their existence from government through welfare, disability, or employment are more likely to vote for continued government agendas that continue or increase their reliance on the government. This leaves fewer people in a position to vote out inappropriate government legislators that may be supportive of unethical or unconstitutional agendas. We have seen just that with the current administration that has made dependence on the government easier than ever to achieve with the knowledge that government dependents will continue to support the status quo. That "status quo" is currently facilitating a government that desires to completely control the public rather than merely govern it.

Control comes in a myriad of forms. The more power we voluntarily give to the government the more privacy we surrender and the more control we subject ourselves to. The Democratic Party once referred to as the party of the people, has been hijacked by socialists dead set on furthering their socialist agenda in the United States. Admittedly, the Republicans were responsible for the Patriot Act which completely destroyed the right to privacy in this country. However, the Obama Administration continued and expanded on the Patriot Act rather than let it play out and sunset as it was scheduled. On May 26, 2011 Obama signed a four year extension of the Act allowing for roving wire taps, searches of business records and surveillance of "lone-wolf" individuals who may be suspected of terrorist related activity. While the Patriot Act may have been justifiable immediately after the 911 terrorist attacks, the Democratic Party has taken advantage of its worst provisions to continue domestic spying and mass control. Unfortunately the American Socialist movement is also intimately tied to the United Nation agenda and creating a one world government. Herein lays the value of electronic weapons and surveillance technology in the hands of those who wish to exert control.

The exponential growth of government jobs and the welfare state has also duped millions of people into the realm of government control. Various government agencies have spent billions of dollars on studying human behavior and human interaction. They are well aware of the effects of providing an easier path of existence than hard work and individual responsibility. The more money you contribute to assisting the helpless, the more helpless you create. Those receiving entitlements from the government tend to vote in favor of government programs critical to further those entitlements regardless of how destructive those proposed agendas may be. Currently, the Democratic Party heavily relies on this voter behavior to continue their position of power and thus their socialist agendas. Many Republicans are in this same boat. If it appears I am focusing mostly on the Democrats, it's because currently they tend to lean more toward Socialism than most Republicans. However, one can look at the voting registry in Congress and see that Republicans and almost all Democrats voted against oversight of the NSA and its domestic spying programs. This list can be found by searching the congressional record and those legislators should not be re-elected when they run for continued office.

The lack of governmental oversight with regard to the NSA, disability, welfare, and immigration policy is not a haphazard mistake on the part of the federal government. It has been intentionally done to pave the road to perdition, making the path to total control much easier to reach with little to no resistance by the populace. The bloodless conversion to Socialism in America relies on making the people comfortable in their subservience so they continue electing the individuals who continue their entitlements. Many of them, and certainly those resisting the change, may be the victims of electromagnetic control measures to help facilitate the desired belief that the government should be in control. It appears to be working. The words of JFK seem so distant in today's society where most people seem to be of the opinion that government should be taking care of them. Perhaps most of the population is already being controlled and the government is singling out those resistant to if for more severe electronic harassment. As ominous as that sounds, one of the scientists that worked on several CIA mind control projects has said just that. Another scientist who worked on naval microwave projects, long ago stated that every brain on the planet could be controlled by electromagnetic weapons. It's not science fiction or futuristic; it is happening currently.

I have included this chapter because one cannot properly addresses electromagnetic control measures without addressing control measures in general and how we have been led to our current dilemma. Certainly, I have illustrated the United States government's lack of oversight in human experimentation over the years and our dismal record on human rights protection. However, years of lack of oversight over illegal immigration and welfare entitlements have also bolstered the number of people who will mindlessly follow the government agenda of total control to maintain their comfort level. We have sat idly by as the current generation of people thirty and under have been dumbed down and brainwashed in public schools. We have turned a blind eye to the rampant abuse of welfare by able bodied Americans who should be working and contributing to society rather than relying on the tax dollars of those who do. We have watched the government absorb many private industries completely and severely restrain others with bureaucratic red tape and taxes to the point that the government is now America's largest employer. There is no such thing as a free lunch. What the government may be offering in one hand is extracted with the other at a heavy cost. We have allowed a political climate to form in this country in which the government can do whatever it wants to the populace with impunity.

I'll paraphrase Winston Churchill from his speech prior to the United States entering WWII which I find extremely applicable today. In trying to coax America into assisting the war effort against Nazi Germany, he essentially pointed out three options of battle. One can fight when there is a good chance of victory without bloodshed, one can fight when there is a perilous chance at victory with high costs or one can fight once there is little choice because it is better to die in battle than live as a slave. We now live in a society where this government is experimenting on the public with electromagnetic weapons for the sole purpose of control. We have long been subjected to the peering gaze of the NSA over all of our communications and seen those who attempt to politically resist get immediately struck down. We have allowed the government to financially control almost half of the population financially through subsidies and the other half through predatory taxation. With regard to Churchill's options for battle, where do you think we are? In October 2013, in a combined NBC/Wall Street Journal poll, 60% of Americans polled wanted to fire and replace every single member of Congress including their own representatives. Hopefully this is a sign that Americans are beginning to awaken out of their apathy that allowed government to grow into the tyrannical beast that it has become. However, I fear it may be somewhat late of awakening to fight the battle with assured victory and little bloodshed. This beast has already been in preparation of this day coming. We have seen that in the numbers of coffins purchased by FEMA and the guns, ammunition, and military vehicles acquired by the Department of Homeland Security as well as the full spectrum surveillance by the NSA. Something tells me they are preparing for a lot more than another hurricane hitting the gulf coast!!

The next chapter will focus on surviving electronic harassment but there are other control factors that must be fought alongside the experimentation with electromagnetic weapons. The entire system has to change; otherwise the government will eventually admit that they possess this technology and continue using it and find a way to justify its use under the guise of national security. Most of our privacy has already been usurped in this manner without much objection from the public. We need sweeping governmental and societal change in order to prevent and control further invasions into our most basic right to be left alone and have privacy of thought. I am not referring to the sweeping change that Barack Obama had in mind for the United States either. So far, that has been change for the worse and has accelerated our decline into Socialism. Socialists will rely heavily on electromagnetic control technologies to further advance their agenda and create a socialistic one world government once America falls further into the abyss. As I have stated before, Socialism sounds good on the surface due to the inequalities of capitalism; however, socialism only makes us all equal in our misery.

First, we must teach individual responsibility in our children again. The government should not be a safety net for those unwilling to work to support themselves. If you have chosen to not learn a skill or pursue education to make yourself occupationally viable then you should not expect the government to raise your standard of living to those that have. Life is not fair and it never will be! Although it is ones constitutional right to have as many children as they would like, it should not be the taxpayers legal requirement to support children you know you cannot afford. Children born into welfare tend to remain on welfare into adulthood, engage in criminal activity more so than non-welfare children, have lower IQs, have higher illegitimacy rates, and higher school dropout rates. A Cato Institute study noted welfare programs for the poor incentivized the very behaviors that are most likely to perpetuate poverty. More oversight into fraudulent welfare programs and much more emphasis on individual responsibility are needed to combat the slavery of welfare.

Secondly, we need to demand ethical behavior on the part of our elected leaders. If legislators tend to lean toward socialistic values, than they should not be elected. A good start would be removing the legislators who voted against increasing oversight over the NSA after their domestic spying scandal got major media coverage. Term limits for Congress people would also be a good thing. Perhaps we should make serving as a legislator voluntary as it is on many municipal types of council. No one should spend a lifetime serving in Congress; the impetus for corruption over the years is far too great and inescapable. Our system of government has changed in such a way that, for the most part, only the wealthy can afford to run for office. This is not government of the people by the people, but rather a handful of elite continually re-elected to control the mass of worker bees within the constraints of the hive-mind that has been designed for us. The Tea Party candidates, mostly pro-Constitutionalists, have fought this status quo which has caused their vilification in this media. Equally hated and ridiculed by both Republicans and Democrats, perhaps they are the breath of fresh air our system truly needs. Only time will tell.

Once we begin to remedy the causes of a government that has been allowed to control us, we can begin to focus on the specifics of nonconsensual experimentation with electromagnetic weapons. The European Union is listening to NSA Whistleblowers and the organization ICAACT through Parliamentary proceedings. Perhaps the United States Government will have little choice but to follow suit, once the "cat is out of the bag" so to speak. Thousands of letters to our current administration and Congress regarding electronic harassment have been largely ignored by Republicans and Democrats alike who are an integral part of the agenda of control. I hope that the combination of mounting pressure from the European Union and the installment of more constitutional minded legislators into the United States government will eventually bring electronic harassment to the forefront of Congress as it did in the Rockefeller Commission and the Church Committee hearings. As a matter of fact, in September 2013, the European Union Parliament's LIBE Committee on Civil Liberties, Justice, and Home Affairs recently heard testimony from several individuals regarding NSA overreach. NSA whistleblower Thomas Drake and Kirk Wiebe as well as cyber security specialist Jacob Appelbaum all testified as to the seriousness and extreme overreach of the NSA into our personal privacy. Jacob Appelbaum recommended to the LIBE Committee that the United States government move forward with another Church Committee type proceeding in order to give Congress the power of the subpoena to access classified documents from the NSA, CIA, and FBI to get a more honest sense of just how far these agencies have gone across the line. According to Appelbaum, "the old argument of security versus privacy is mute. We have privacy through security and total loss of privacy is not privacy for the sake of security."

Too often at speaking engagements or on radio shows that I am a guest on, I hear comments like, "I'm not a criminal so I have nothing to worry about if they spy on me." It saddens me to hear such ignorance among the people because the definition of what is considered criminal may change from administration to administration. By definition, the Tea Party Republicans are not criminals or terrorists, yet they were targeted by the IRS and a multitude of other agencies. Journalists are not terrorists but the Obama Administration has exponentially increased the number of journalists targeted for exposing the harsh realities of his administration. The Obama Justice department has prosecuted more government whistleblowers under the 1917 Espionage Act than all prior administrations combined. In 2007 in a speech regarding the war on terror, Obama promised no more wiretapping, no more tracking United States citizens for protesting the war, and no more National Security Letters. For those unfamiliar, a National Security Letter is a legal instrument used by the FBI to circumvent a judge and subpoena to demand specific information about an individual from organizations or communication companies. It allows the FBI access to phone records, transaction records, and emails and contains a gag order preventing the recipient from discussing that the letter was even issued. It goes against every Constitutional right that we have and has been used extensively under the Obama administration. So, do you still feel safe about being spied on because you are not a criminal? If so, enjoy the shade under the pergola, have a refreshing drink and behold the pale horse; he should be trotting by shortly.

CHAPTER 16
Prise de Fer

"Eye for eye, tooth for tooth, hand for hand, foot for foot, burn
for burn, wound for wound, stripe for stripe..."

–Exodus 21:24-25

We have a long, painful road ahead of us as far as reforming our government and re-introducing morality, ethics and respect for individual rights in the United States. We have allowed ourselves to be herded like cattle and thus we have continued to be treated as such. There are small pockets of resistance developing like the Tea Party, the Libertarian Party and other community action groups whose goal is to restore constitutional law in the daily activities of the federal government. The hope is to return to a government of the people, by the people, for the people as President Lincoln so poetically described in his Gettysburg address. One must remember that the Gettysburg address came about due to revolution in this country regarding the principle of human equality. Approximately 750,000 men, roughly 2% of the United States population at that time, died in the fight to abolish slavery. Currently we are all slaves to a subtly tyrannical government with a questionable amount of fortitude to fight it. We have been dumbed down by public education, enslaved by entitlements, controlled by taxation and bureaucracy, subjected to privacy invasion and experimented on like lab animals without consent. It's time that we take the blade and counter-attack within the scope of our political ability if we can, with insurrection if we must.

For those unlucky enough to have been chosen, against their will, to be part of the current experimentation with directed energy weapons, I will divide some information on combating it into two parts. First will be group suggestions and secondly individual survival tips will be covered. The reason for dividing this information into two sections is so it is clear that group techniques will be needed to combat the issue and individual survivor tips are for self-preservation and not necessarily aimed at controlling the problem as a whole. Both are important but I believe that group efforts at exposing the crime as a whole will ultimately bring about the best form of individual preservation. Those readers unaffected by nonconsensual experimentation should continue reading as the number of victims voicing these complaints is growing exponentially both in the United States and abroad. The chance that this technology will affect you or a family member in the near future is probably close to 100%. As we now know, the NSA is collecting virtually all of your personal communications and the logical next step would be an attempt at mass control of the population, assuming it's not already being done. Therefore, the outcry for exposure of this technology should be coming from all of humanity, not from those already victimized alone.

Group Counter Attack

Ethical Government

We must return our government to an ethically based Constitutional abiding government. The power of the vote and the ability to remove and re-elect new leaders is one of our more powerful weapons. I realize that sometimes it seems futile to worry about elections and voting but when large groups of people feel this way and fail to exercise their right to vote it does have consequences. Obviously anything can happen in a United States election! We have seen our current President elected twice with no verifiable background, no history of achievement in the private sector, and a history of socialistic beliefs in his upbringing. Regardless of party affiliation we must begin to elect leaders based on their willingness to defend the Constitution and all of its tenets. A good start to that end would be to not re-elect the Congresspersons that voted against increasing NSA oversight and voted for ratification of the United Nations Arms Treaty which would severely limit American citizens' rights to bear arms. The lists of Congress people that should be elected out of office because of their constitutional beliefs can be found through a cursory Google search regarding which Congress people voted for the United Nations Arms Treaty and against NSA oversight. Any legislator that is of the mindset that full spectrum surveillance of the citizenry and the allowance of a United Nations gun ban to supersede our 2nd amendment right to bear arms is tolerable must never be in office at any level of government. This mindset leans itself directly to the belief that the public must be controlled and disarmed. You will notice that all of the Senators that voted in favor of the United Nations Arms Treaty are Democrats, but none of them are Democrats from Texas!

Term Limits

According to The Congressional Research Service the average length of service in the United States House of Representatives, as of 2013, is 9.1 years. The average length of service in the United States Senate is 10.2 years. However, there are a number of legislators that have spent a good portion of their adult lives in office. The office of the Presidency is limited to two four year terms to avoid the establishment of a tyrannical executive office; however, no such limits exist for Representatives or Senators. At one time there were fundamental differences in the two political parties which somewhat kept each other in check, so term limits were probably less necessary. However, the two major parties are now two wings of the same foul creature that is growing exponentially and wanting to exact more and more control. Therefore, term limits will insure periodic governmental change when the constituency may be too entitled, ignorant, or controlled to know when their candidate should be put out to pasture.

Critics of term limits will argue that it is the democratic right of a candidates' constituency to elect their favorite as often as they choose to. However, there is no question that anyone spending a lifetime in Congress is more likely to support the status quo rather than the ethical high ground with regard to legislation. Big government will always pass legislation to continue growing even bigger government. Legislators that know their time in service is limited will be more likely to enact legislation that is less controlling of the private sector due to their inevitable return to the private sector. It is my belief that term limits in Congress would eventually lead to more effective legislation against nonconsensual experimentation as well as more legislation in favor of the right to privacy as defined in our own Bill of Rights.

Community Education

Educational efforts have been ongoing for some time both through human rights organizations dealing with electronic harassment as well as individual victim's blogs. The problem with this type of community education is that it mostly targets the part of the community already affected by electronic harassment and searching google for remedies to their harassment. This type of educational effort is essentially akin to preaching to the choir. Despite the number of internet references to electronic harassment, the major media has largely ignored the topic. Recently, in response to the number of mass shootings in the United States, there has been some major media coverage questioning whether mind control is at play. Investigative journalist Alan Jones wrote several excellent articles in the Washington Times Communities section of their website regarding the connection between Aaron Alexis and electronic harassment. Hopefully other journalists will follow his lead as the numbers of "controlled" shooters continue until the government hears the public outcry for gun control that they are hoping to hear.

Several billboards have been erected that state "Big Brother is watching you." to further the community awareness campaign regarding electronic harassment. Amazingly, these billboards were up and attracting attention well before Edward Snowden broke the news that indeed, Big Brother has been watching. The billboards include the phone number for Freedom from Covert Harassment and Surveillance, a human rights organization that offers information to potential sufferers of electronic harassment as well as educational information to victims and non-victims alike.

Other upcoming attempts at community education include a motion picture based on my first book, A New Breed, which will be a drama based on a true story. The Discovery Channel has expressed an interest in doing a series on targeted individuals which will hopefully come to fruition. More approaches at community awareness will hopefully be brought forward by human rights organizations or individuals. The importance of community awareness cannot be understated. As more people are educated about electronic harassment we will see less tragedy as a result of victimization due to poor understanding of the phenomenon by relatives and employers. Over time, the outcry from non-victims along with victims of electronic harassment for government disclosure of the technologies used may actually have a better chance of succeeding. Furthermore, once the existence of these technologies becomes common knowledge as well as their effects, it will not be feasible for them to be used as successfully against an enlightened public. Non-victims who understand the implications and reality of this technology will be less apt to send their loved ones to psychiatrists who, wittingly or unwittingly, may contribute to their victimization. Also, as non-victims grow in their understanding about this crime, hopefully they will add additional voices to the outcry for disclosure and appropriate oversight regarding the testing and use of these weapons.

Medical Education

As the number of people voicing complaints of nonconsensual exposure to electromagnetic weapons increases, so will their visits to their respective physicians. For too long these people have been turn-key referred directly to psychiatrists who typically misdiagnosis them as mentally ill despite an overwhelming amount of information about this issue online. Fortunately more and more physicians are beginning to recognize that something is afoul with our government and its lack of legislation regarding nonconsensual experimentation. However, psychiatrists do not seem to be following suit. We need an intense program of educational efforts aimed at community based psychiatrists regarding electronic harassment. At the top of both the American Psychiatric Association and the Canadian Psychiatric Association, I believe that they are well aware of the nonconsensual experimentation being done. After all, they were actively involved in the earlier research that brought us to where we are today. The community psychiatrists working in the trenches appear to be largely ignorant of their field's checkered past and are likely to blindly follow the guidelines put forth by their national associations. Well-designed educational efforts may be able to reach some of these ground-level psychiatrists who are currently seeing most of the people voicing complaints.

With the threat of psychiatric diagnosis removed, a significant amount of bite would be taken out of this technology's ability to destroy the lives of those exposed. The success of this technology is almost always hinged upon its ability to marginalize the victim through a false psychiatric diagnosis.

Individual Protection

Efforts at individual protection from electromagnetic weapons are an ongoing quest for both individuals who may be getting nonconsensually victimized and the government itself. The DoD has long had a call for scientific abstracts from the civilian sector regarding protection from electromagnetic weapons for both personnel and equipment. The International Society for Optics and Photonics, or SPIE, has a current call for abstracts regarding remote sensing for surveillance to be discussed at its meeting in Baltimore. It appears that many of these electromagnetic weapons have been developed by most industrialized nations without any reliable way to protect themselves from them. That being said, recommendations on individual protection is based upon extrapolation of current research done on the physiologic effects of electromagnetic fields as well as research done with alleged victims on nonconsensual experimentation in vivo. What is covered in this book is what has been found to be successful in lessening the effects of exposure to chronic electromagnetic fields.

We know from multiple studies that chronic exposure to RF can cause cognitive decline, premature aging, cataracts, decreased sperm counts and tissue damage. These efforts are thought to be secondary to decreased melatonin levels, increased heat shock proteins and increased levels of ornithine decarboxylase (ODC). Increased ODC levels are the most concerning due to its tumor stimulating effect and these levels may vary depending on how the signal is modulated. Melatonin has many functions in the human body other than sleep reduction as most people are familiar with. Melatonin has a very powerful anti-oxidant effect in the human body and chronic exposure to electromagnetic fields decreases its ability to function. Heat shock proteins are present in normal cells but increase with electromagnetic field exposure through non-thermal effects. These proteins serve as chaperones to other proteins and aid them in transport through cellular compartments. They also help in scavenging proteins that have been unfolded improperly or had their structure altered which may render them fatal to the cell in which they reside. It appears that the chronic exposure to electromagnetic fields causes increased free radical production which, in turn, probably causes the cascade to other cellular changes that are seen as detrimental to the human body. Therapy with potent free radical scavenges does seem to mitigate some of the physical efforts of chronic exposure. If one were to find themselves under chronic exposure, a combination of alpha lipoic acid 600mg/ day, vitamin D3, 2000 iu/day, sublingual glutathione 50 mg/day and melatonin would be of great benefit to preventing the drastic effects of increased free radicals on the body.

Many victims contact me or other organizations that deal with electronic harassment searching for shielding recommendations. In 2012 ICAACT (International Center Against Abuse of Covert Technologies) was allowed use of a Faraday cage in Belgium to conduct testing which included RF scanning of known targeted individuals and unaffected individuals as a control group. The testing was recorded on video and a report was generated which can be found on the ICAACT website. The Faraday cage was certified in December of 2011 and rated to be effective between 9 KHz and 18 GHz. The results were significant. The group of individuals who were known victims tested positive for RF transmissions within the cage while the unaffected control group showed no transmissions emanating from their bodies. Moreover, the positive group did report a subjective increase in their sense of well-being while within the cage with a relative absence of effects that they had previously complained about. Although this is only one experiment with a small population, I believe it does anecdotally lead one to believe that a well-constructed, research level Faraday cage does offer some protection from exposure. While it would be infeasible for one to live their life within a Faraday cage, perhaps a smaller cage could be constructed with similar parameters for in-home nocturnal use to combat sleep deprivation which is common among all victims. ICAACT is currently working on development of an affordable, compact Faraday cage for individual use based upon current finding of the study. Moreover, several other research organizations have begun expanding on our experimental protocol with a larger population of experimentees; hopefully they will find similar results. Other common sources of shielding have shown promise for protecting electronic equipment, such as computers, but have largely failed in lessening the effects on human beings.

Many victims complain of microwave based physical attacks which may include full body heating but more often is reported as attacks at specific points on the body. We know from directed energy studies that microwave beam propagation is somewhat impeded by salt water. Studies have shown that microwave beams tend to skip across the surface of the ocean after their propagation through the atmosphere from aerial based sources. For individuals reporting certain areas of the body being attacked with microwave energy, covering those areas with bags filled with salt water at the same tonicity as sea water may offer a measure of protection.

The second most common question heard from victims of electronic harassment involves microchip removal. Certainly, there has been an abundance of research done with a myriad of materials used to invent micro-implants for human tracking and physiologic manipulation. However, surgeons cannot remove what they cannot see on some type of medical imaging. Despite over a decade of complaints of electronic harassment, very few implants have been identified or removed. The most renowned case of implant removal involved an inventor named Bob Boyce in Georgia. After inventing a self-charging battery circuit using energy from the environment, Boyce was allegedly drugged and chipped by a former NSA employee. Two Verichips were removed from Mr. Boyce's body at Fannin Regional Hospital in Georgia. At least one of the areas in his body that was chipped displayed tissue changes of malignant melanoma, a known sequelae of this type of chip. Due to this case, I believe it is wise for victims to be RF scanned and have medical imaging done to rule out implantation. However, thousands of victims have been medically imaged with very few implants found which alludes to the targeting being done another way, possibly through EEG recognition, DNA resonance, facial or body recognition or an as of yet unidentified method. It is my belief that overcoming this will not be as easy as identifying an implant and removing it.

Because these weapons have been designed to specifically target the human control nervous system, much of our effort has been focused at rendering the brain unresponsive to exposure. As mentioned previously in the book, Robert Malech patented an apparatus for remotely monitoring the brain in 1974. It included targeting the brain with two dissimilar frequencies which would stimulate the brain and transmit an interference frequency from which the EEG could be decoded. The invention was devised with the purpose of monitoring pilots to determine their state of wakefulness or disorientation. I believe that much of the current targeting is being done with a variant of this technology which has been exponentially improved upon since 1974.

If one looks at the current research being done on brain-computer interfacing (BCI), you will immediately notice that the research is being done to determine the difference between BCI in the synchronous versus the asynchronous EEG. The human brain typically has a synchronous EEG, although it may appear as asynchronous in some pathological states. Malech's patent also induces asynchrony by forcing the brain to entrain two different waveforms simultaneously which is why an interference frequency is transmitted by the brain as it grapples with two different frequencies of entrainment. Most of the research points to better brain-computer interfacing with an asynchronous EEG versus an EEG that is synchronous. Brain-computer interfacing is the cornerstone of electronic harassment.

A great deal of this research is being done or funded by the Institute of Electrical and Electronics Engineers (IEEE), the organization that recommends limits on RF exposure to the government. Moreover, the IEEE also retains a special fund for financing certain United States members to do fellowships in Congress. According to the IEEE, "this provides a unique educational experience to our members as well as advice and assistance to policy makers." The IEEE is intimately involved with President Obama's Brain Initiative and the "Big Brain Project" at McGill University in Montreal. They have already completed a terabyte map of the brain to understand how it functions computationally. One must remember that McGill University was a major player in MKULTRA. The Human Connectome Project is another Brain Initiative program being done at the Washington University School of Medicine in St. Louis. Its focus is to give insights into which parts of the brain act in concert to do seemingly simple tasks such as recognize a face.

Based upon current research findings it would appear logical that attempts at maintaining a synchronized EEG would offer some protection from induced asynchrony for possible nonconsensual brain-computer interfacing. In a number of victims we have used binaural beat programs, used while sleeping through ear phones, to attempt to synchronize the EEG. Two binaural beat programs have been utilized. Neuro-Programmer 3 for Windows based laptops and the Brainwaves Application for Apple products like the iPad. The Brainwaves App by Bonzai Labs is the more user friendly of the two. The results have been significant. Nearly all persons using a nightly binaural beat program have reported a decrease in audio harassment followed by a decrease in physical symptoms. More research needs to be done in this arena as it does appear that synchronizing the EEG and thus stopping the transmission of an interference frequency offers protection. It is my belief that if one can stop or limit the entrainment of exogenous frequencies and the corresponding interference frequency that many of the symptoms of electronic harassment will fade away.

Much more research needs to be done within the private sector with regard to protective mechanisms against intrusive neurological weapons. The information I have relayed in this chapter is merely the tip of the iceberg as far as what needs to be done. Unfortunately, the majority of the research being done currently is looking at ways to improve BCI, not protect the human brain from it. Moreover, the research is mostly government funded now through Obama's Brain Initiative or covertly funded through the government through third party research organizations like the IEEE. It will require private sector financing to adequately fund protective technologies research to combat the ever more intrusive, growing neurological technologies that lie on our horizon as a species.

CHAPTER 17
Conclusion

The twenty-first century has brought a number of technological advancements that have the potential to benefit humanity as well as destroy it. If one were to go back through history books from the past, that opening statement would be similar to other statements made by writers concerned with advancements made in their respective eras. However, the concerns we have in this era are distinctly unique in that we are now facing technology with the capability to enslave us and rob the individual of their most basic right, the right to free will. Our creator granted humans the ability to exercise free will. It has always been the individual's choice to choose good or evil and reap the consequences of either. Unfortunately, we now live in an era in which our governing bodies have developed technologies that enable them to manipulate the central nervous system, thus manipulating free will. This will be a difficult battle to fight as we have allowed government to grow so large and unrestricted that the majority of legislation it passes is solely meant to perpetuate its own growth. An entire generation of people has been duped into believing that government intrusion is a good thing and that we cannot survive without government assistance. It was never intended to be this way. Thus, we have allowed the government to become our keeper, controller and enslaver.

In addition to some of the remedies I've mentioned earlier in this book, there are some basic tenets that I believe would put us back on the right track. First, able-bodied people should provide for themselves. Fewer people on welfare means less government control and a free market economy does offer the best chance of financial success, despite what liberals would have you believe. It should be explicitly illegal for any government agency to experiment on the public here or abroad without informed consent. This sounds basic, but no such laws exist within our current legislation on human experimentation. This is a travesty and makes the United States appear hypocritical in its complaints about human rights violations in other countries. We must elect our leaders based upon their ethical and moral character. The people must continue to hold its leaders feet to the fire to enact legislation that is in the best interest of humanity or their heads to the noose when they don't.

We must have intelligence agency oversight. Regardless of whether you believe Edward Snowden is a traitor or a savior, he did us a favor by substantiating what most of us had figured out long ago. The most recent revelations include the "Dropout Jeep" software implant for the Apple iPhone 5s that enables the NSA to remotely monitor, manipulate, and steal data from your iPhone. I informed a number of targeted individuals about this several years ago. The software does require physical contact with the phone for installation. In addition, it has come to light that the NSA has also been intercepting laptops ordered online in order to install spyware on them before they are delivered to the purchaser. It is time that we demand our legislators enact intense oversight over the NSA and the myriad of other intelligence agencies that have so far, operated with impunity. I have heard the arguments for apologists for the intelligence community that if one is not up to "no good" then they have nothing to worry about. That is not a good argument for me or the American

Public. What the government considers "no good" may change on a day to day basis and a belief that is tolerable one week may be considered radical the next. The definition of good or bad is a situational definition based on which state department is defining it at the time. We have seen this with the continued targeting of the Tea Party by the IRS.

Difficult times lie ahead for our country as more and more people tire of a government bent on controlling us through full spectrum surveillance and deployment of electromagnetic weaponry. As I see it the federal government is responsible for maintaining a military for our protection and enacting regulations to ensure that our air and water are clean. As a people we must use our power at the election booth to begin restricting the size and intrusiveness of the federal government. It is the only way to preserve this country for future generations so that they can enjoy the freedom and privacy that those of us over fifty enjoyed in our youth. Sadly, if this cannot be done peacefully through legislative circles I can see a time in the near future when desperation will lead to the shedding of blood in our streets to enact the changes that are needed. According to H.L. Mencken, "The most dangerous man to any government is the man who is able to think things out...without regard to the prevailing superstitions and taboos. Almost inevitably he comes to the conclusion that the government he lives under is dishonest, insane, and intolerable."

References

<u>Documents and Articles</u>

Basile, Kathleen, Swahn, Chen, Saltzman, "Stalking in The United States," American Journal of Preventative Medicine, Vol. 31, Issue 2, pgs. 172-175, August 2006

Londgrebe, Michael, Association of Tinnitus and Electromagnetic Hypersensitivity: Hints at Shared Pathophysiology, Dept. of Psychiatry, Psychosomatics, and Psychotherapy, Univ. of Regensburg, Regensburg, Germany, March 27, 2009.

Saunders R.G., Jefferys J.G., "A Neurobiological Basis For ELF Guidelines," Health Phys., 2007 Jun: 92C6):596-603.

"New Surveillance Tech Tracks Every Move," Dove Summers, NBC7 San Diego, 6/29/2013.

"Obama unveils brain mapping project to unlock mysteries," David Jackson, USA Today News, 4/02/2013.

"Resisting the Surveillance State," Reason.com, Steve Chapman, July 29, 2013.

"New Research: Electro pollution can cause diabetes (type-3)," Mike Ranger, Natural News.com, June 10, 2013.

Center for Disease Control and Prevention, Natural Diabetes Fact Sheet, 2011.

The HIV/AIDS Epidemic in the United States, Henry J. Kaiser Family Foundation, May 22, 2013.

"In his words: Emails Alexis sent raise questions on government urveillance," Alan Jones, Washington Times Communities, October 24, 2013.

"What are the ELF Weapons Alexis and other Americans fear?" Alan
Jones, Washington Times Communities, October 24, 2013.

"Effects of pulsed electromagnetic fields on cognitive processes—pilot
study on pulsed field interface with cognitive regeneration," Maier,
R, Acta Neural Scand. 2004 Jul; 110C1) 46-52.

"Calcium channel blockade alleviates brain injury induced by long
term exposure to an electromagnetic field," Soliman, Hala, Journal
of Applied Biomedicine 6: 153-163, 2008.

"Non-Thermal Biomarkers of exposure to radiofrequency/
microwave radiation," Ivancica Trosic, Institute of Medical Research
and Occupational Health, Zagreb Croatia, June, 2011.

"Soviet Directed Energy Weapons Perspectives on Strategic
Defense," March, 1985

"Capturing with EEG the Neural Entrainment and Coupling
Underlying Sensorimotor Synchronization to the beat." Nozaradon,
Sylvie, cereb.cortex (2013) Oct.9, 2013.

"Gov't Knows Best? White House creates 'Nudge Squad' to shape
behavior," Maxim Lott, Foxnews.com July 30, 2013.

"White House Forming 'Nudge Squad' to influence Americans to
see it President Obama's way," NYDailyNews.com, Leslie
Larson July 31, 2013.

"NSA broke privacy rules thousands of times per year, audit finds,"
Julie Tate, Barton Gellman, The Washington Post, August 15, 2013.

"Review of US Surveillance Programs to be let by panel of
Intelligence insiders." Paul Lewis, The Guardian, August 22, 2013.

U.S. Patent 51356,368 "Method and Apparatus for Inducing Desired
States of Consciousness" March 1, 1991. Robert A. Monroe,
Interstate Industries, Inc.

"Governments employ 20 percent or more of workers in nine states,"
The Business Journals, G. Scott Thomas, May 14, 2012.

Reference Documents and Papers:

"Mind-Control Toys: The Force Is with You," TIME, Alexandra
Silver, Thursday Feb 19, 2009.

Steinschneider, M. "Temporal Encoding of the Voice Onset Time
Phonetic Parameter by Field Potentials recorded directly from
human auditory complex," International Journal of

Neurophysiology, 1999 Nov; 82 (5):2346-57.

Davis, KE, Coker L., Sanderson M., 2002, "Physical and Mental Health Effects of Being Stalked for Men and Women," Violence and Victims 1 (4).

"Remote detection of human electroencephalograms using ultrahigh input impedance electric potential sensors," Applied Physics Letters, Issue date: 21 October 2002.

Ackerman, M. Alfred, Ayers, Curtis W., Haynes, Howard D., Ultrasonic speech translator and communications system, Martin Marietta Energy Systems, Inc. USPTO, appl.no 08/329,899 July 23, 1996.

Baum, K., Catalono, S., Rand, M., (2009), Stalking Victimization in the United States. Washington D.C.: National Institute of Justice.

Braud, W. and Schlitz, M., (1989) Remote Mental Influence of Electrodermal Activity, The Mind Science Foundation, San Antonio, Texas.

Vasiliev, Leonid, (1962) Experiments in Mental Suggestion. Leningrad State University.

Vasiliev, Leonid, (1963) Experiments in Mental Suggestion. London: Institute for the Study of Mental Images.

Vasiliev, Leonid, (1976) Experiments in Distant Influence. New York:Dutton.

Persinger, M.A., Ludwig, H.W., and Ossenkepp, K.P., "Psychophysiological effects of extremely low frequency electromagnetic fields: A Review," Perceptual and Motor Skills, 1973, 36, 1131-1159.

Persinger, M.A., "Classical psychophysics and ELF magnetic field detection." Journal of Bioelectricity, 1985, 4 (2), 577-584.

Persinger, M.A., and Makaree, K., "Possible learned detection of exogenous brain frequency electromagnetic fields: A case study." \ Perceptual and Motor Skills, 1987, 65, 444-446.

Faden, R.R. Final Report, Advisory Committee on Human Radiation Experiments. Washington, DC: U.S. Government Printing Office, 1995.

The Central Intelligence Agency's Search for Records on Human Radiation Testing, Government Printing Office, 1994.

Department of Health and Human Services, Search for Records of Human Radiation Experiments, Government Printing Office, 1995.

Department of Defense Activities on Human Radiation Experiments

Review, Government Printing Office, 1995.

Fact Sheet for Advisory Committee on Human Radiation Experiments: NASA Review of Human Radiation Experiments, Government Printing Press, 1994.

Vangelova, K., Israel, M. and Mihaylou, S., The effect of low level radiofrequency electromagnetic radiation on the excretion rates of stress hormones in operators during 24-hour shifts." Cent. Evr. J. Public Health 10(1-2): 24-28, 2002.

(ISTC G-989) Complex Study of Neurological, Cardiological and Hematological Correlates of Extremely Low Frequency Electromagnetic Field Exposure in Animals. University of Washington/ Department of Bioengineering, National Institute of Public Health, 2008.

Nielsen, P.E., Effects of Directed Energy Weapons, United States Air Force, 1994.

Pinneo, L.R. and Hall, J., Feasibility Study For Design of a Biocybermetic Communication System, Stanford Research Institute, Prepared for DARPA, Contract DAHC-15-72-C-0167, August 1975.

Malech, R.G., Apparatus and Method for Remotely Monitoring and Altering Brain Waves, US Patent 3951134, 4/20/1976.

*If you loved this book, would you please
provide a review at Amazon.com?*

Printed in the USA
CPSIA information can be obtained
at www.ICGtesting.com
LVHW041731230724
786273LV00009B/281